A Life Well Lived, the Remarkable Story of Hugh S. Thompson, Governor of South Carolina

Hugh T. Harrington

Hugh T. Harrington
3801 Village View Dr, Apt 1125
Gainesville, GA 30506
hharring@charter.net

Dedication

To educators, particularly those teaching history, who shape not our past but our tomorrows.

(His signature)

Acknowledgements

I particularly want to thank my grandmother, Caroline Beaumont Thompson (daughter of Governor Hugh and Elizabeth Thompson), who would tell me history stories, when I was a child. Also, my father, William H. Harrington, who taught me to "feel" the history. My cousin, William Glasgow Thompson, who reminded me of the importance of our history both now and for the future. My wonderful uncle, Hugh T. Harrington, with whom I enjoyed so much history as we dug into our shared past together. I regret that none of these are here to read the story they helped to write.

Many thanks to my friend, historian, and author, James N. Littlefield, who encouraged me, as well as provided invaluable insights and suggestions. Historian John L. Smith, Jr. provided sage advice. My distant cousin Louise Thoman was enthusiastically supportive as was cousin Emily Iland. Joan Harrington Clayton has been inspiring and has also supplied real hope that future generations will find our history interesting and worthwhile. In addition, Joan has become a repository for many archival artifacts.

Other family and friends have provided support enabling me to stay the course during times when the project seemed doomed. My sincere thanks to you all.

My greatest help has been from my wife, Sue the magician, who has innumerable times brought order out of chaos and made the impossible possible. Without her none of this would have been possible. She is the rock.

All errors, and doubtless there are errors, are mine and mine alone.

Contents

Introduction

In writing this book, I intend, as well as I can, to set the record straight regarding what Hugh Smith Thompson did and, when necessary, what he did not do. It should be understood that Hugh S. Thompson is my great grandfather. Sometimes when people look back at their family's past they may personalize and perhaps feel guilty when they learn that their ancestors, their own flesh and blood, were murderers or thieves, were involved, for example, in the forced removal of the Cherokees on the Trail of Tears, owned slaves, or fought for a cause that may be considered offensive. My ancestors, and perhaps yours, have done all of that and more. It is not logical for us to assume any guilt on ourselves for what our ancestors may have done, as we were not alive at the time and had no control over any of those past events. On the flip side, neither should we pridefully pound our chests whenever we discover ancestors who performed admirably by today's standards. History just "is what it is": an honest accounting of events. Certainly, valuable lessons can be learned, but personal guilt or bragging rights should be curbed whenever personal ancestries are under review.[1]

It can be said that Hugh S. Thompson was an important member of the family. He was also important in a broader sense in American history as he had a role to play in South Carolina and on the National stage. I see my responsibility to be a preserver and presenter of the facts. I have accumulated a good deal of information, and it is my responsibility to see that it does not disappear, and I will pass along the facts as well as I can. It is the reader's responsibility to accept, reject or perhaps dig into the story further. It would also be appreciated if the reader would pass the history to the current, as well as future, generations.

---

[1] My thanks to my friend the historian, teacher and novelist, Jim Littlefield, for his insights on historical objectivity.

Hugh Thompson was a strong, and vocal, proponent of education for all, Black and white, as the only way to a brighter future, not just for South Carolina but for the entire nation. His views were visionary at that time in the North as well as in the South. He said, "The learning of the few is despotism. The learning of the many is liberty." And "We want a school system that is good enough for the rich and cheap enough for the poor." Also, "we shall have to be taxed either for ignorance or education. Every dollar taken from the schools will go to the support of the jails, penitentiaries, and poor-houses." He was a man well ahead of his time...and our own.

The *New York Times* wrote of him, "...a South Carolinian by the accident or good fortune of birth, Gov. Thompson is an American," and "there is no State in the Union in which he will not be at home." He had risen above regionalism. He was an American yet still championed southern history and continued to honor its heroes.

A lifelong Democrat, he rose above party politics when he endorsed Republican William McKinley over the issue of the gold standard, which he felt was more important than the party to which he had been devoted throughout his life. As such he is a good role model for American politicians today to follow.

When considering the life of Hugh S. Thompson, and his wife Elizabeth "Lieze" Clarkson Thompson, one should keep in mind the famous speech of Theodore Roosevelt, *Citizenship in a Republic*, popularly known as "The Man in the Arena." The Thompsons were in the Arena and, fortunately, came out with "the triumph of high achievement." Theirs is the story of the Man in the Arena:

> *It is not the critic who counts; not the man who points out how the strong man stumbles, or where the doer of deeds could have done them better. The credit belongs to the man who is actually in the arena, whose face is marred by dust and sweat and blood; who strives valiantly; who errs, who comes short again and again, because there is no effort without error and shortcoming; but who does actually strive to do the deeds; who knows great enthusiasms, the great*

devotions; who spends himself in a worthy cause; who at the best knows in the end the triumph of high achievement, and who at the worst, if he fails, at least fails while daring greatly, so that his place shall never be with those cold and timid souls who neither know victory nor defeat.[2]

Hugh Thompson and Theodore Roosevelt would become good friends in the last decade of the 19th century. Roosevelt spoke of him saying, "I can say that I have never, in political, business, or social life, met an abler or more high-minded man." And "He is an absolutely fearless and manly man, conscientious to a degree, with great tact in dealing with men."

On Nov. 10, 1901, Theodore Roosevelt, the President of the United States, extended an invitation to Hugh Thompson to dinner at the White House, which was accepted. On April 9, 1902, President Roosevelt was at a dinner given in his honor in Charleston. He said,

Just twelve years ago when I first went to Washington to take part in governmental work I was immediately thrown into singularly close contact and intimacy with a South Carolinian. It was my good fortune to work with him for three years, and for the nine years since and for as long as I shall continue to be in public life, it will be to me ever a spur to try to do my whole duty to the Republic because I have been thrown intimately in contact with as fair and as high-minded a public servant as this country has ever had, my old friend, your former Governor, Hugh Thompson.

Roosevelt also wrote of his friend saying, "I never met a braver, gentler, or more upright man."

On his deathbed, Hugh Thompson asked that a letter he had received that day from President Roosevelt be read aloud to him. They were friends until the end.

---

[2] Roosevelt, Theodore, Speech at the Sorbonne, Paris, France, April 23, 1910.

This is the man, my ancestor, the respected friend of President Theodore Roosevelt, who I grew up knowing only that he was, in the hazy past, the Governor of South Carolina. There is a very great deal more to his story. And it is a good story.

Hugh T. Harrington
Gainesville, Georgia
October 1, 2024

Chapter 1
In the Beginning

Hugh Smith Thompson played a significant role in the history of South Carolina in the second half of the 19th century. He graduated from The Citadel in Charleston in 1856, became an educator, and returned to The Citadel to teach. He led The Citadel cadets in battle during the Civil War. After the War he returned to teaching. He became South Carolina Superintendent of Education (1877-1882), followed by two terms as Governor of South Carolina (1882-1886). In 1886, he left South Carolina for the position of Assistant Secretary of the U.S. Treasury (1886-1889) in Washington. D.C. and later served as United States Civil Service Commissioner (1889-1892). In 1892 he joined the New York Life Insurance Company in the position of Comptroller. His service, particularly during the Civil War in South Carolina, has become clouded with legend and perhaps wishful thinking. Therefore, it is the intention here to present a more accurate record of his activities.

Hugh S. Thompson was born in Charleston, January 24, 1836, to Henry Tazewell Thompson (1812-1866) and Agnes Smith Thompson (1816-1879) of Greenville, South Carolina. His 19-year-old mother had gone to the home of her mother, Eliza Catherine Martin Smith (1788-1861) in Charleston for the birth of her first child. The location of the home may be at a corner, which corner is unknown, of Bull and Rutledge Streets. Hugh was the first of nine children. Eliza Catherine Martin Smith's husband, Hugh Smith (1782-1826), had been a merchant and architect in Charleston.[3] The names Hugh and Smith have carried through the family for 200 years.

---

[3] Hugh Smith designed St. Andrew's Hall located on Broad Street in the now empty lot on the west side of John Rutledge House Inn, 117 West Broad St. It burned to the ground in a massive fire Dec. 11, 1861. There is plaque on the original fence at 119 W. Broad St.

Hugh Thompson grew up on his father's farm located at the base of Paris Mountain in Greenville, SC. In 1929 this land became Hillandale Golf Course. In 1930, a bronze plaque mounted on a large stone, commemorating the site as his boyhood home, was placed at the site (34° 54.302' N, 82° 24.856' W), now the corner of Hillandale Rd. and S. Parker Rd., three miles SSW of Paris Mountain. The historic marker and the stone no longer exist. Hugh's uncle, General Waddy Thompson, Jr. (1798-1868), had a large home atop the mountain.

General Waddy Thompson, Jr. was Brigadier General of the 1st Brigade of South Carolina Militia in 1832 and was referred to as General for the remainder of his life. Gen. Thompson was a 2-term U.S. Congressman from 1835 to 1841 and minister to Mexico in 1842.[4]

From his home on Paris Mountain, Waddy Thompson, Jr. could look down on the farm of his brother Henry Tazewell Thompson. Henry, and son Hugh, would wig-wag semaphore messages back and forth to Waddy Jr. on Paris Mountain.

Hugh Thompson attended schools in Greenville. In 1852, he entered The Military College of South Carolina, commonly known as The Citadel. First year students attended the Arsenal Academy in Columbia. The following three years he was at The Citadel in Charleston. He graduated in 1856. In February, at The Citadel, he delivered "Washington's Farewell Address" at the "Annual Oration." [5] On November 21st, he gave a commencement address, "In what does true national greatness consist?" at the Hibernian Hall, 105 Meeting Street. The newspaper wrote that the subject "gave full scope for the exercise of the young speaker's oratorical powers, and he improved the occasion to much advantage, and fully came up to the expectations of the audience."[6]

---

[4] Much of HST's early history as well as that of Waddy Thompson, Jr. is from Hennig, Helen Kohn, *Great South Carolinians of a Later Date* (Chapel Hill: The University of North Carolina Press, 1949).
[5] "Celebration of the 22nd February at The Citadel Academy," *Charleston Courier*, February 22, 1856.
[6] *Charleston Mercury*, November 22, 1856, p. 1.

Hugh S. Thompson as a Citadel cadet

After graduation Hugh obtained an assistant teacher position at the Columbia Male Academy, which was located on the northeast corner of Laurel and Pickens Streets in Columbia (34° 00' 41.16" N, 81° 01' 50.44" W).

Elizabeth Anderson "Lieze" Clarkson

On April 6, 1858, at the age of 22, this young man from a relatively modest background married Elizabeth Anderson Clarkson (1840-1909),[7] the beautiful 17-year-old daughter of Thomas Boston Clarkson (1809-1879),[8] one of the wealthiest

---

[7] She was named for her grandmother, Elizabeth Anderson Harris (1773-1849), wife of William Clarkson (1760-1825).

[8] Thomas Boston Clarkson (1809-1879) controlled vast areas of cotton plantations mainly in Richland County, SC, southeast of Columbia. He was a large planter with a large slave workforce. After the Civil War he lost his properties to taxes and foreclosures. His father, William Clarkson (1760-1825), was a factor (the man of business for the large planters), as well as a planter. Wm. Clarkson owned until his death, when his son took over, the family home on Bull Street, Charleston, which is now used as office space

men in the state. Known as "Lieze" to her friends, this remarkable young woman would not only be his life-long companion but also his rock during the many hard times that they would share in the future. The marriage took place at Trinity Episcopal Church (now Cathedral) in Columbia. The story of how Hugh managed to make such a brilliant marriage has unfortunately been lost to history.

Also in 1858, Hugh was appointed to the position of professor, with the rank of 2nd Lieutenant, at the Arsenal Academy in Columbia, where he taught French and Belles-Lettres, the art of fine, literary writing.[9] The Arsenal Academy was located on the grounds of what is now the Governor's Mansion, the northwest corner of Laurel and Lincoln Streets (34° 00' 30.23" N, 81° 02' 36.36" W). In February 1865, the army of General William T. Sherman burned most of Columbia and the Arsenal Academy. The only structure remaining is now the current Governor's Mansion. Hugh and Lieze lived in that building when he was an assistant professor and 20 years later as Governor.

In 1859, Hugh was promoted to 1st Lieutenant at the Arsenal Academy in Columbia.[10] He remained at the Arsenal Academy until August 1861. July 6, 1859, Hugh and Elizabeth's first child, Henry Tazewell Thompson, named after Hugh's father, was born in Columbia.[11]

---

by the College of Charleston. Thomas Boston Clarkson is the gr-gr-grandson of theologian and author, Scots Presbyterian minister of Ettrick Scotland, Thomas Boston (1676-1732).

[9] Thomas, John Peyre, *The History of the South Carolina Military Academy* (Charleston: Walker, Evans & Cogswell Co., 1893), 93. This book should be considered as a primary source in that the author, a member of the Citadel class of 1851, was an officer of The Citadel during the period discussed in the book and includes statements from other officers who were also present.

[10] Thomas, John Peyre, *The History of the South Carolina Military Academy*, 99.

[11] Henry Tazewell Thompson (1859-1932) would attend Union College in Schenectady, NY, become a lawyer and historian, as well as Lt. Col., 2nd South Carolina Regiment in the Spanish American War and serve in the National Guard for 40 years.

When discussing southerners prior to 1865 it is often wondered if they owned slaves. To be clear Hugh S. Thompson and his wife, Elizabeth Clarkson Thompson, owned slaves and literally all their ancestors owned slaves going back in time as far as can be traced. It was legal and was accepted as the norm at that time.

The 1860 Census indicates Hugh owned 3 female slaves with ages of 18, 20 and 22.[12] He may not have been in a financial position to purchase them. However, his wealthy father-in-law, Thomas Boston Clarkson, who had 9 male and 25 female slaves working at his mansion in Columbia, probably gave his son-in-law and daughter the three slaves. Similarly, Hugh and Elizabeth's son, Thomas Clarkson Thompson (1860-1938) wrote that "...my grandfather gave her [the slave, Nancy DeSaussure, Thomas Clarkson Thompson's Black nurse] to me at my birth [Sept. 21, 1860]."[13]

Hugh and Elizabeth Thompson's second child, Thomas Clarkson Thompson (1860-1938), was born September 21, 1860, at the Arsenal Academy in the building that is now the Governor's Mansion.[14]

---

[12] 1860 Federal Slave Inhabitants, City of Columbia, Richland County, South Carolina, July 28, 1860.

[13] Thompson, Thomas Clarkson, *The Narratives of Thomas Clarkson Thompson, 1860-1938*, edited and annotated by Hugh Thompson Harrington. (Gainesville, GA, privately printed, 2019) 9, 19. Available at archive.org and Amazon.com. T.C. Thompson wrote that the nurse was the slave, Nancy DeSaussure. After the war she was the wife of Robert Brown Elliott, Attorney General of the State of South Carolina.

[14] Thomas Clarkson Thompson is best remembered for being the mayor of Chattanooga, TN 1909-1915. The Children's Hospital in Chattanooga was named for him. See also: Thompson, Thomas Clarkson, *The Narratives of Thomas Clarkson Thompson, 1860-1938*, edited and annotated by Hugh Thompson Harrington. (Gainesville, GA, privately printed, 2019) 9, 19. Available at archive.org and Amazon.com.

Chapter 2
Civil War Service with The Citadel Cadets

It is an unfortunate consequence of the computer age, where a myriad of sources of information are readily available at the fingertips, that unreliable information can be found as easily, perhaps more easily, as can dependable information. The history of Hugh S. Thompson has suffered from a multitude of online sites, probably emanating from the unverified *National Cyclopedia of American Biography*, that asserts, erroneously, that he was "captain of a battalion of state cadets which fired the first gun of the Civil War, January 9, 1861, upon the *Star of the West*."[15] The *Star of the West* was a United States supply ship attempting to reach the besieged Fort Sumter located in Charleston harbor.

South Carolina had seceded from the Union on December 20, 1860, and had demanded that the United States troops occupying Fort Sumter in Charleston Harbor surrender and evacuate the fort. That demand had been refused. South Carolina troops had then laid siege to the fort.

This *National Cyclopedia*, from which the erroneous accounts of Hugh Thompson derive, is described as unverified, old data from shelf list cards and was copyrighted in 1928.[16] The exact wording may vary, but the erroneous statements appear in a wide variety of sites including *Wikipedia*, findagrave.com, Historical Marker Database, National Governors Association, *History of South Carolina* edited by Yates Snowden, and numerous others. Invariably, these sources do not include Thompson's actual combat experience on

---

[15] *The National Cyclopedia of American Biography*, vol. 24, New York: James T. White & Company, 1935.

[16] See reference to the *National Cyclopedia of American Biography* at Library of Congress: https://www.loc.gov/item/2005681973/. Accessed August 4, 2024.

December 7, 1864, along the Charleston and Savannah railroad at Tulifinny Creek, nor his other military activities.

The definitive history of The Citadel's first 50 years was written by Colonel John Peyre Thomas in his *History of the South Carolina Military Academy* in 1893. John P. Thomas was a member of the class of 1851, an English professor, a Superintendent of the Arsenal Academy, and Captain of Company B (the Arsenal cadets) in combat at Tulifinny Creek. When The Citadel reopened in 1882 after the war, he was named Superintendent. He was also a member of the Board of Visitors and named State Historian in 1887. When John P. Thomas was doing the research for his book, Hugh Thompson wrote him: "Of the service of the Cadets in repulsing the *Star of the West,* in January, 1861, and of the officers of the Academy in the reduction of Fort Sumter in April of that year, it is not necessary for me to speak, as you know more of those matters than I do."[17]

The reason John P. Thomas knew the matters better than Hugh Thompson was because Thompson was at the Arsenal Academy in Columbia until August 1861 and therefore did not have first-hand experience regarding the *Star of the West* or the firing on Fort Sumter. Since he did not fire on the *Star of the West*, he did not carry the burden of beginning the maelstrom of the Civil War, as some propose.

On January 9th Major Peter F. Stevens, Superintendent of The Citadel, as well as professor of astronomy and engineering, gave the command to open fire on the *Star of the West*, which was passing the cadet battery on Morris Island. Cadet George E. Haynsworth, class of 1861, not Hugh Thompson, pulled the lanyard firing the first round across the bow of the ship.[18]

After the war excitement of April 1861, the cadets and their officers would assist in drilling newly formed companies and regiments in the Charleston area. Many cadets resigned from The Citadel to join units heading for combat. Thus passed

---

[17] Thomas, John Peyre, *The History of the South Carolina Military Academy*, 208.

[18] Bond, O.J., *The Story of the Citadel*, 1936, 50-51. Thomas, John Peyre, *The History of the South Carolina Military Academy*, 443.

the first year of the war with a combination of classroom study and drilling of recruits.

On August 28, 1861, the governing body of the South Carolina Military Academy, called the Board of Visitors, met at Columbia and issued a resolution appointing Hugh Thompson Secretary pro tempore of the Board of Visitors. At the same meeting, he was promoted from 1st Lt. to Captain and transferred to The Citadel as professor of Belles-Lettres and Ethics. The rank would be effective October 1st, and he was to report for duty at The Citadel on the same date.[19]

On March 7, 1862, the Executive Council of South Carolina passed a resolution exempting the The Citadel officers and cadets from militia service or the Confederate draft. In April the Confederate congress passed a Conscription Act covering almost all white men between 18 and 35. Hugh was 26.[20] The Citadel cadets and military staff were considered a stand-alone unit of the Confederate army.

On June 1st, Union troops landed on James and Johns Islands near Charleston. The Citadel cadets were ordered to James Island along with eight field pieces. They did not participate in any combat. When the cadets had been ordered out by Maj. Gen. John C. Pemberton, commander of the

---

[19] Thomas, John Peyre, *The History of the South Carolina Military Academy*, 111. The Citadel, the Military College of South Carolina, "Minutes of the Board of Visitors of The Citadel, 1861," *The Citadel Archives Digital Collections*, accessed May 7, 2022, https://citadeldigitalarchives.omeka.net/items/show/376.

The meeting minutes of the Meeting of the Board of Visitors of August 28, 1861, was hand-written by Hugh S. Thompson, which includes his appointment to position of Secretary pro tempore of the Board of Visitors, promotion to Captain and transfer to Charleston on October 1, 1861.

The Citadel, located on the North side of Marion Square, on Meeting Street in Charleston, was three stories when Hugh was a professor there. The fourth story was added later. In 1922, The Citadel moved to its present location abandoning the old building which, in 2024, is a hotel. The new campus includes Thompson Hall, which was named for Hugh Thompson, and houses the Department of Mathematics and Computer Science.

[20] Baker, Gary, *Cadets in Gray* (Columbia, SC, Palmetto Bookworks, 1989), 49-50.

Department of South Carolina, it was thought by Major James B. White, superintendent and commander of The Citadel, that Gen. James Jones, Chairman of the Board of Visitors in Columbia, should be notified.

Capt. Hugh S. Thompson was sent to Columbia to inform Gen. Jones. Jones wanted the cadets withdrawn. On June 17, 1862, the cadets were ordered to return to The Citadel and to their studies yet hold themselves in readiness for duty. Thirty-six cadets, determined to fight in the war, left The Citadel and formed their own company known as the Cadet Rangers or Cadet Company. Initially, The Citadel considered them as suspended and later categorized them as having been expelled. The cadets considered themselves as patriots intent on doing their duty.[21]

Hugh Thompson, as Captain, remained at The Citadel. Throughout the war The Citadel cadets did guard duty at government warehouses in and around Charleston. They also guarded prisoners and provided military honors at funerals of officers killed in battle.[22]

Union forces captured the northern end of Morris Island on July 10, 1863. The cadets were ordered to turn out and assembled at the wharves for transport to Morris Island. However, before they embarked, Gen. Roswell Ripley ordered them to return to The Citadel as they would not be needed. The cadets returned, with great regret, to their guard duties. In early October they were given a furlough. Upon their return they resumed guard duties.[23] One can imagine their disappointment.

---

[21] Baker, Gary, *Cadets in Gray*, 54-56. Thomas, John Peyre, *The History of the South Carolina Military Academy*, 210.

[22] Baker, Gary, *Cadets in Gray,* 61-68.

[23] Thomas, John Peyre, *The History of the South Carolina Military Academy*, 211. John Peyre Thomas includes a letter written by Hugh S. Thompson, on pages 208-212, which describes the movements of the cadets from November 1861 to the end of the war. Unfortunately, Hugh Thompson does not speak of the action along the Charleston and Savannah Railroad writing, "...it is needless for me to speak to you, who were an eye witness to the gallantry of the cadets..." John Peyre Thomas, as captain, commanded Company B, the cadets from the Arsenal Academy at Tulifinny

Beginning in August 1863, Charleston was under artillery fire from Union batteries on Morris Island. The southern side of Charleston absorbed the majority of this fire. The shelling became a fact of life that was tolerated since little could be done to prevent it. By the end of the war the city was heavily damaged.

In late May or early June 1864, the cadets were ordered to James Island as an attack was threatened. The cadets performed picket duty in the heat and exposure of summer weather but did not see action other than occasional shelling. It is therefore unlikely that Hugh Thompson was with his wife when she gave birth to another son, John Means Thompson,[24] on June 14th in Columbia. In the fall, the cadets were granted furloughs.

When they returned to duty in October 1864, there was Yellow Fever in Charleston. They were ordered into camp near Magnolia Cemetery outside of town and then to Orangeburg to avoid the disease.[25]

The cadets were at Orangeburg when they were ordered to return to Charleston. On December 5th Gen. James Jones, Chairman of the Board of Visitors, stated that The Citadel building was no longer safe due to the continual bombardment of Charleston.[26] For the remainder of the war the cadets would serve in the field. There would be no more academic studies. At long last the cadets were going into combat.

The Citadel cadets formed Company A commanded by Captain Hugh S. Thompson. They were joined by the Arsenal cadets, Company B, commanded by Captain John Peyre Thomas. The two companies, a total of 343 men combined as

---

Creek. Captain Hugh S. Thompson commanded Company A, The Citadel cadets at Tulifinny Creek.

[24] John Means Thompson (1864-1934) worked in real estate throughout his life. In the Spanish American War, he was 1st Lieutenant, Co. K, 71st NY Volunteers at San Juan Hill.

[25] Thomas, John Peyre, *The History of the South Carolina Military Academy*, 211.

[26] Thomas, John Peyre, *The History of the South Carolina Military Academy*, 176.

the Battalion of Cadets, were commanded by Major James B. White.[27]

The cadets were needed to reinforce the troops engaged in defending the Charleston and Savannah Railroad.   This connection between Savannah and Charleston was vital as it carried troops and supplies between the cities. The countryside through which the railroad ran was heavily wooded swamps requiring the railroad to be built upon causeways with bridges over the creeks and streams. The Union forces in Beaufort and Hilton Head had attempted to cut the railroad line on several occasions, but since Southern reinforcements could be hurried by rail to threatened points, the Union forces had been unsuccessful.[28]

At midnight December 3rd the Cadets formed in the quadrangle of The Citadel and were ordered to prepare to march in 30 minutes. With Enfield rifles, knapsacks and blankets, but no tents, they marched to the tune of a fife and drum to the Charleston and Savannah depot on the southern side of the Ashley River where they boarded boxcars for the train ride to the small town of Coosawhachie.

Early on the morning of the 4th they disembarked at Pocotaligo, sixty miles from Charleston and 4.75 miles from Coosawhachie. They marched down the railroad track 2 miles to the bridge over Tulifinny Creek. They camped in the rain, without tents, along the railroad embankment.[29]

Captain Thompson wore the standard grey Confederate uniform with green facings. Until 1863, The Citadel officers

---

[27] Thomas, John Peyre, *The History of the South Carolina Military Academy*, 206. Baker, Gary, *Cadets in Gray*, 203-219. The first-year students at the Arsenal Academy were younger and their ranks enhanced by parents hoping that cadets would avoid conscription into the regular Confederate forces. The Citadel cadet ranks, Company A, were thinned as students had resigned to form the Cadet Rangers or other Confederate units.
[28] Baker, Gary, *Cadets in Gray*, 134.
[29] Baker, Gary, *Cadets in Gray*, 136. Colonel O.J. Bond, *The Story of the Citadel* (Richmond, VA, Garrett and Massie, 1936) 76. Includes, Coffin, George M., "My Recollection of Fight at Tulifinny Creek, South Carolina, in December 1864" written in 1929. Bond also includes the report of The Citadel commander Major James B. White.

16

had worn old Federal-style blue uniforms. The cadets wore gray wool and cotton uniforms with cartridge boxes held in front and behind by crossed straps. Percussion cap boxes were on the right side of the waistbelt. A bayonet scabbard was on the left. In comparison to the veteran troops assembled along the railroad, some of whom were barefoot, they were splendidly dressed.[30]

Upon their arrival late on December 4th, the Cadet Battalion camped on the southern side of the railroad trestle[31] crossing Tulifinny Creek.[32] This location is 1.7 miles, by railroad, north of the little crossroads of Coosawhachie. It is 0.7 miles, overland, northwest from the nearest point on I-95 but is inaccessible except by walking the railroad tracks, which is not recommended.

The cadets put out pickets. After a supper of bacon and hardtack the cadets bedded down for the night. December 5th was spent awaiting orders.[33] The railroad bridge was vital because if it was destroyed by the Union army, communication between Charleston and Savannah would be cut.

The Cadet Battalion was not the only Confederate force defending the railroad line. Companies F and B, 47th Georgia Regiment, part of Capt. W.K. Bachman's Artillery battery with four twelve pounders, and the 1st SC Regulars, all under the command of Major J.B. White, were present.[34]

On the morning of December 6th, the enemy, commanded by Maj. Gen. John P. Hatch, debarked at Gregory's Plantation on the Tulifinny River and marched northwest on the dirt road

---

[30] Baker, Gary, *Cadets in Gray*, 136.

[31] GPS 32° 37' 16.96" N, 80° 54' 09.15" W.

[32] GPS 32° 37' 17.05" N, 80° 54' 09.33" W. This precise location is inaccessible by car or foot. The area is only a few feet above sea level and is swampy. It is .7 miles NW from the nearest point on I-95.

[33] Baker, Gary, *Cadets in Gray*, 139.

[34] *The Charleston Mercury*, December 9 and 16, 1864. Heriot, Robert, "Fighting in South Carolina," *Confederate Veteran*, vol. XXX no. 11, Nov. 1922, p. 415. Heriot, formerly a cadet at the Arsenal Academy, who resigned to enlist in the Confederate army, was present during the action as a member of Bachman's Battery. Hugh Thompson likely did not see Robert Heriot nor recognize him as a first cousin of his wife.

now designated as State Road S-27-172, toward the dirt country road between Savannah and Charleston where I-95/US-17 is now. They met light resistance from various Confederate forces. The sound of the skirmishing 3 miles away was clearly audible to the cadets waiting for orders at the bridge. Ordered at the double-quick toward the fighting, they reached the scene of battle only after the Federal troops had withdrawn. Major White ordered the cadets back to the railroad trestle where they lay in the rain during the night attempting to get some sleep.[35]

During the night, gunfire from the picket line caused the entire Battalion of Cadets to form in line of battle. The Federal troops a mile away did not advance. No one got much sleep that night.

At sunrise, Thursday December 7th, a skirmish line composed of Captain Thompson's cadets of Company A and three companies of the 5th Georgia infantry advanced toward the enemy. Major White was in overall command. The Arsenal cadets, Company B, followed in reserve.

It was cold with a light frost as the skirmishers moved forward. While they were receiving fire from the enemy, skirmishers went forward pushing the enemy back through creeks, lagoons, woods, broom grass, swamps, and across the dirt road approximately where I-95 is now. They exchanged fire with several enemy regiments that had formed a strong line. They proceeded to within 100 yards of a Federal battery when they were flanked by strong opposition. Receiving grapeshot and heavy rifle fire they withdrew.[36] To the veterans the cadets appeared, in their new uniforms, as if they were on dress parade firing in disciplined volleys.

The cadets joined the 47th Georgia behind an embankment. Major White, on horseback, rode behind the cadets calling to them "Steady! Let them come well up" and cautioned them to remain concealed behind the natural breastworks. The enemy came out of the swamp into a field with bayonets fixed. Maj. White shouted, "Attention battalion! Ready!...Aim!....FIRE!"

---

[35] Baker, Gary, *Cadets in Gray*, 139.
[36] Baker, Gary, *Cadets in Gray*, 142.

At the order "attention battalion" the cadets leaped to their feet. The command "fire" unleashed the muskets of the cadets. The Federal line broke. The Georgians and the cadets advanced after them.[37]

At one point, cadet private Joseph Barnwell picked up an enemy haversack, which contained some fresh bread. He called to Captain Thompson, "Captain, they feed those fellows better than our people do us for see this bread and we have only hardtack and not much of that." Captain Thompson laughed. At that instant a bullet struck Barnwell above the knee. Immediately thereafter Lt. Amory Coffin, Assistant Professor and Adjutant of the Cadet Battalion, was severely wounded when struck in the forehead by an enemy bullet. Company A had one cadet killed outright. Besides Barnwell, another cadet was severely wounded. Four other cadets from Company A received minor wounds.[38]

After skirmishing for three hours, Company A was nearly out of ammunition. The Company retired to the rear to resupply. Their place in the line was taken by Company B, the Arsenal cadets.[39]

As in all battles, glimpses and isolated details were remembered by the participants. A former cadet, Robert Heriot, now a member of Bachman's battery, recalled that "the cadets fought as if on dress parade. Their firing could be distinguished above the roar of battle by the regularity of their discharges."[40]

John Peyre Thomas, commander of Company B, wrote "This was the first time the Battalion of Cadets met the enemy, but their conduct was such as to excite the commendation of the veteran troops, by whose side they fought, and to call for the approval of the Commanding General, as well as the Colonel commanding the expedition. Every cadet acted with

---

[37] Baker, Gary, *Cadets in Gray*, 143-144.

[38] Baker, Gary, *Cadets in Gray*, 142. Thomas, John Peyre, *The History of the South Carolina Military Academy*, 207-208.

[39] Baker, Gary, *Cadets in Gray*, 144.

[40] Heriot, Robert, "Fighting in South Carolina," *Confederate Veteran*, vol. XXX no. 11, Nov. 1922, p. 415.

conspicuous gallantry and showed that the discipline of his academy had made him a thorough soldier for the battlefield."[41]

On December 8th the Federals strengthened their position. The cadets did the same, throwing up breastworks parallel to, and on the east side of, the railroad.[42]

The Battalion of Cadets was engaged on December 9th when the enemy advanced toward the railroad embankment. However, the action was to the right of the cadet position at Tulifinny bridge; therefore, the cadet involvement was only partial. Most of the day had been spent marching and countermarching.[43]

The cadets lived on short rations, usually one meal per day, without tents, and as cadet Farish Carter Furman wrote in a letter on December 18th, "To give you some idea of the life we lead I will tell you that I have not pulled off my clothes for fourteen days." Water for drinking, and other purposes, came from a ditch along the railroad embankment.[44] In mid-December, Arsenal Academy cadet Waddy Thompson, a cousin of Hugh S. Thompson, somehow managed to accidentally shoot himself with his rifle.[45]

Between action on December 7th and Christmas, the cadets would drill new recruits in non-Citadel companies. Occasionally, they were interrupted by artillery fire from the Federals. The Federal troops did not capture the railroad line until General Sherman arrived in January.

---

[41] Thomas, John Peyre, *The History of the South Carolina Military Academy*, 207.

[42] Baker, Gary, *Cadets in Gray*, 148.

[43] Thomas, John Peyre, *The History of the South Carolina Military Academy*, 207.

[44] Baker, Gary, *Cadets in Gray*, 149.

[45] Baker, Gary, *Cadets in Gray*, 150. 17-year-old cadet Waddy Thompson was a 1st cousin once removed of Captain Hugh S. Thompson. His father was William Butler Thompson and grandfather, General Waddy Thompson, Jr. He was from Greenville, SC. After the war he was a physician, dying when he was 35 years old. He is buried at Christ Episcopal Church cemetery in Greenville, near Hugh S. Thompson's father, Henry Tazewell Thompson.

On December 25th the cadets were ordered to James Island where they remained until Charleston was evacuated on February 17, 1865. They encamped near Battery Number 2, close to Legare's Crossroads and Secessionville, where they performed picket duty as part of the Brigade of Stephen Elliott. Here they enjoyed having tents.

Captain Thompson contracted typhoid fever in January while on James Island. He wrote that he was sent to "one of the hospitals in Charleston, and from there to Columbia, where for many days I was under the treatment of Doctors Gibbes and Chisolm. Although unable to walk, my friends succeeded in getting me out of Columbia a short time before Sherman entered. I rejoined my command at Greenville, remaining with it until its disbandment after the surrender of Gen. Johnston's army."[46] The identities of these "friends" are unknown.

It is almost certain that Hugh was cared for at the home of his wealthy father-in-law, Thomas Boston Clarkson (1809-1879). T.B. Clarkson's mansion, formerly the home of Governor James Henry Hammond, was a magnificent structure with 36 columns thirty feet tall located at the Northwest corner of Bull and Blanding Streets.[47] Hugh's wife, Elizabeth "Lieze" Clarkson Thompson, and their children had been living there since 1863 having left Charleston seeking safety. She gave birth at her parent's home to her first daughter on January 21, 1863. This daughter, Elizabeth Anderson Thompson, died in Greenville on September 7, 1863, at the age of 7 months.[48]

The Thompsons' second son, Thomas Clarkson Thompson, wrote in the 1930's, "I remember getting off the train at a station once with my mother and I had to step over

---

[46] Thomas, John Peyre, *The History of the South Carolina Military Academy*, 212. This quote is from a letter of Hugh S. Thompson to J.P. Thomas.

[47] St. Paul's Lutheran Church is located on the site of the Clarkson mansion.

[48] My grandmother, Caroline Thompson Harrington (1874-1969), told me that she lost a sister during the war. I had the impression that she died while fleeing Sherman but that clearly was not the case. Perhaps, she died as a result of another non-combat, but wartime, cause. Or, she may have died of some non-war related injury or medical issue.

dead Confederate soldiers who were lying on the platform waiting to be moved and buried."[49] Life, even away from active combat, must have been difficult and frightening, especially for young children.

In mid-February 1865, the vast and powerful army of General William T. Sherman was approaching Columbia. Everyone knew what Sherman's army had done in Georgia. Atlanta had been destroyed by fire, and the army cut a wide path of destruction from Atlanta to Savannah in the famous, or infamous, March to the Sea.

Columbia was defended by a completely inadequate force that could not hope to prevent, nor even delay, the city from being taken by the enemy. Inevitably, the Confederate military, the government and the citizenry sought to leave town before it was too late. The few outbound trains were overwhelmed. The roads were packed with frightened refugees, many on foot, frantically fleeing north in hopes of safety. Panic ensued as the incoming Union artillery fire spurred them on. Without law and order, looting in the city became widespread. Numerous fires of various origins spread through Columbia.

Lieze Thompson faced a desperate situation. Her sick husband had been carried out of the city. However, she was left with her three sons, five-and-a-half-year-old Henry Tazewell Thompson (1859-1932), four-and-a-half-year-old Thomas Clarkson Thompson (1860-1938) and 8-month-old John Means Thompson (1864-1934). She had to make some critical decisions with potentially dire consequences. Could she stay in Columbia and risk herself and her children to the mercies of the enemy? No. Facts, and rumor, had forever stained Sherman's army with a fearsome reputation for brutality and wanton destruction. If she decided to flee, how and where would she go?

Twenty-four-year-old Lieze Thompson was resourceful and tough. She decided she would refugee, if she could, to

---

[49] Thompson, Thomas Clarkson, *The Narratives of Thomas Clarkson Thompson, 1860-1938*, edited and annotated by Hugh Thompson Harrington, Gainesville, GA, privately printed, 2019, p. 17.

Greenville, South Carolina, to the home of Hugh's father, Henry T. Thompson, over 100 miles away.

On February 16th, the day before Sherman burned Columbia, she made the incredible decision to give her son Thomas Clarkson Thompson to a slave, William DeSaussure (aka Blacksmith William), with instructions to take her little boy to her father-in-law's home in Greenville. She would make the same journey with her sons Henry and John. Apparently, she and her two boys would travel, by unknown means, to Greenville independently from Thomas and William DeSaussure. Perhaps this was done with the thought that spreading the risk might better the chances that one or more of the boys would make it through.

The burning of Columbia

The night of February 17th would never be forgotten by anyone in Columbia. Young Thomas Clarkson Thompson wrote, "I was four and one-half years of age and the burning of this house [the Clarkson mansion] was my first distinct recollection."[50] Wherever the fleeing refugees were on the road they would see the light in the sky at night behind them from the

---

[50] Thompson, Thomas Clarkson, *The Narratives of Thomas Clarkson Thompson, 1860-1938*, edited and annotated by Hugh Thompson Harrington, Gainesville, GA, privately printed, 2019, p. 5.

fires as Columbia burned. In the day the smoke was visible for many miles. Along with most of the city, the mansion of Lieze's parents would be burned that night.

Ruins of the Clarkson mansion

The epic journey of the white child and the devoted Black man, William DeSaussure, took an astonishing 13 months. It is the sort of tale of which a novel, or movie, could be made. However, many might not believe it to be true. Very regrettably all the details of this dramatic story have been lost to history as Thomas Clarkson Thompson was too young to remember much, and nothing was written down.   That William DeSaussure brought the little white boy through the panic of thousands of refugees fleeing Columbia, the war-ravaged countryside, and chaotic post-war South Carolina to reach Greenville is an epic adventure, of over a year, that stirs the imagination. Sixty years later Thomas Clarkson Thompson wrote in tribute to William DeSaussure, "this slave never left me for a moment."[51]

---

[51] Thompson, Thomas Clarkson, *The Narratives of Thomas Clarkson Thompson, 1860-1938*, edited and annotated by Hugh Thompson Harrington, Gainesville, GA, privately printed, 2019, p. 5.

Complicating their journey was that Lieze did not remain long in Greenville. General Robert E. Lee surrendered on April 9th and General Joseph Johnston on April 26, 1865, effectively ending the war. Lieze returned to Columbia, where she was joined by her husband, now that the War was over. They lived on the second floor of the Columbia Male Academy.[52] When William DeSaussure and young Thomas arrived in Greenville, they found that Lieze had gone back to Columbia, so they had to make their way back to Columbia to join them.

When young Thomas Clarkson Thompson first saw his mother again, he did not identify her until he saw a mole on her left eyebrow that he recognized.[53] The distress of his mother when her son and William Desaussure seemingly disappeared into the chaos after the burning of Columbia must have been agonizing.

Caroline Thompson

The importance, the lasting impact, of Sherman's destruction of Columbia and South Carolina cannot be overstated. My grandmother, the Thompson's daughter Caroline (1874-1969), who was born in 1874, maintained a hatred for General Sherman, and all things Sherman, throughout her long life. She was a lifelong Episcopalian; yet when I was confirmed in 1964, she refused to attend the service as the officiating bishop was named Sherman [Jonathan

---

[52] Columbia Male Academy likely was spared by the fire as it stood on a broad lot.

[53] Thomas Clarkson Thompson mentions this episode in *The Narratives of Thomas Clarkson Thompson, 1860-1938* by T.C. Thompson, p. 5-6.

G. Sherman, 1907-1989] despite there being no known connection between the bishop and General W.T. Sherman. As it happened the bishop became ill, and another man took his place, so my grandmother attended the service.

When Charleston was evacuated February 17th, The Citadel cadets were part of the brigade of Brig. Gen. Stephen Elliott of Lt. Gen. William J. Hardee's army. Captain Thompson would not have been part of this group since he was recovering from typhoid fever in Columbia. The cadets retreated in front of Sherman's army into North Carolina via Cheraw.

Between Fayetteville and Raleigh, Major White received orders from Governor Andrew G. Magrath to return to South Carolina. The cadets escorted Federal prisoners to Raleigh, then reported to the Governor at Spartanburg, SC, arriving on the evening of March 20th. They numbered 120 men. They camped on the grounds of Wofford College. Major White suggested that The Citadel cadets be furloughed for fifteen or twenty days.[54]

Meanwhile, the Arsenal cadets had arrived at Spartanburg on March 8th and were furloughed for fifteen days on March 10th. Perhaps amazingly, after the 15-day furlough almost all of them returned.[55] At the end of March the Arsenal cadets marched to Greenville where they made camp on the Buncombe Road near Paris Mountain on the Greenville and Columbia Railroad close to Finlay's Bridge. The location was also relatively close to Hugh's father's home. The Citadel cadets joined them soon after.[56]

The cadets were encamped at Greenville when they learned of Lee's surrender on April 9th and Gen. Joseph E. Johnston's surrender on April 26th. The Board of Visitors of The Citadel met in Greenville on April 27th and astonishingly drew up plans for continuing both the Arsenal Academy and The Citadel educational programs. The badly damaged Citadel was

---

[54] Baker, Gary, *Cadets in Gray*, 173, 177, citing letter of March 21, 1865 from Major White to Governor Magrath.
[55] Bond, Col. O.J., *The Story of The Citadel*, 83.
[56] Baker, Gary, *Cadets in Gray*, 177. Bond, Col. O.J., *The Story of The Citadel*, 83.

literally in the hands of the Federal troops, and the Arsenal buildings had been destroyed.

On April 29th The Citadel cadets were granted a furlough.[57] The cadets never reassembled. It would be 17 years, while Hugh was State Superintendent of Education, before The Citadel reopened.

---

[57] Bond, Col. O.J., *The Story of The Citadel*, 85. Baker, Gary, *Cadets in Gray*, 177.

Chapter 3
Post Civil War
The World Turned Upside Down

In August 1865, in a world turned upside down, Hugh Thompson, a civilian again, was back in Columbia at the Columbia Male Academy where he had had his first job as assistant teacher in 1856. Now, he was Principal of the Columbia Male Academy.[58] This institution would informally be known as "Thompson's School." He and his family lived on the second floor of the building with the ruins of Columbia surrounding them. With the end of the war, life had dramatically changed in the South and would never be the same again.

Columbia Male Academy

Also known as Thompson's School

---

[58] Thomas, John Peyre, *The History of the South Carolina Military Academy*, 265.

To say that money was tight for the Thompsons is an understatement. They often were hard pressed even for food. Hunger was real. Perhaps to raise a little cash Hugh Thompson endorsed a book, *Sanford's Arithmetics*, in an advertisement that appeared in *Methods of Instruction* by James Pyle Wickersham in 1865. As "Professor Hugh S. Thompson, Principal Columbia Male Academy, Columbia, S.C.", he wrote, *"Sanford's Arithmetics* are superior to any that I have seen in the fullness of the examples, the clearness and simplicity of the analyses, and the accuracy of the rules and definitions. This opinion is based upon a full and thorough test in the school-room. To those teachers who may examine these *Arithmetics* with references to introduction, I would especially commend this treatment of Percentage and Profit and Loss. No test-books that I have ever used are so satisfactory to teachers and pupils."[59]

Confederate Brigadier General James Conner wrote on August 9, 1865, that Columbia, having been burned February 17-18, 1865 by General Sherman's army, was "such a sight I have never seen. A town of chimneys – nothing else standing. It more than realized all that I had ever read of desolation."[60]

The desolation was more than mere destruction of buildings. The agrarian economy was based on free slave labor and there were no longer slaves. There was also no money to pay for laborers. Cash itself was very scarce. Land ownership was in flux as the owners could not pay taxes so lost the property. The new property owners faced the same problems. Much of the land was farmed by sharecroppers working for a percentage of the yield. White men were mostly barred from holding public office, and most could not vote. The Republican party was in power putting ill-equipped Blacks, along with Carpetbaggers from the north, into public office.

---

[59] Wickersham, James Pyle, *Methods of Instruction*, Philadelphia: J.B. Lippincott & Co., 1865.

[60] Stokes, Karen, "'Contemplating Desolation': the Early Postwar Life of James Conner," *Carologue*, (publication of the SC Historical Society), Winter 2016, p. 17. The full letter is included in Moffett, Mary Conner, editor, *Letters of General James Conner*, Columbia, SC: R.L. Bryan Co., 1950, p.167.

South Carolina lost over 20% of its fighting-age white male population killed during the war. This was the highest rate of any of the former Confederate states. In addition, tens of thousands of returning men were wounded, many disabled permanently. Plus, an incalculable number of men were suffering from what in the 21st century would be termed Post-Traumatic Stress Disorder, or PTSD.

The PTSD also affected civilians including non-combatants and women. An often-overlooked casualty of the war was the large percentage of young women of marriageable age who either lost their husbands to the war or who never married because there were not enough returning men for them to marry. The cataclysm suffered by South Carolina, and other former Confederate states, would continue for generations and was not alleviated until the massive production requirements of World War II seventy-five years later. In many respects the effects of the war are still being felt.

This was the situation that the Thompsons, and countless other families and individuals, faced in post-war South Carolina. It would not be easy. At age 29 Hugh Thompson had lost everything with the destruction of South Carolina and Columbia. Gone too was the fabulous wealth, and mansion, of Elizabeth's father, Thomas Boston Clarkson. Elizabeth and Hugh Thompson were in Theodore Roosevelt's "Arena." They were "marred by dust."[61] Together they strived "to do the deeds" and spend themselves "in a worthy cause." However, they had no way of knowing if they would fail or survive to experience "in the end the triumph of high achievement."

Most of what is known of the life of Hugh and Elizabeth "Lieze" Thompson in the immediate postwar era comes from the narratives of their son, Thomas Clarkson Thompson (1860-1938). These narratives, edited and annotated by their great grandson, Hugh T. Harrington, have been published, in 2019, in a very limited edition as *The Narratives of Thomas Clarkson*

---

[61] See Introduction: Theodore Roosevelt, *Citizenship in a Republic*, popularly known as "The Man in the Arena."

Thompson.[62] The following excerpts, in the words of Thomas Clarkson Thompson, will help give an idea of what the Thompsons, and countless others, faced:

> *In the days immediately following the Civil War food was exceedingly scarce. My father had three pupils whose parents were grocers...*[and the parents] *agreed that my father should take $14 a month in groceries. Where the balance of the food came from, I do not know. My father always kept open house for my mother's brothers, all of whom were planting in the fork of the Congaree and Wateree Rivers. As the brothers all had large families there was scarcely a night that some of them were not in our home. Often, they appeared just at meal time and my mother would say to me, 'When they pass you so and so you must not take any and I will not take any because there isn't enough to go around.' I have often believed that my indifferent health was caused by lack of nourishing food when I was a growing boy.*[63]

> *No supper was ever served on Sunday – I presume as a matter of economy. But they always cooked on Saturdays two great baskets of biscuits which by Sunday were as hard as a rock and nearly always had too much soda. We were given two biscuits each and we ate them like hungry wolves. Perhaps no refined people in the world ever suffered as the southern people did immediately following the war. There never was enough to go around. I can remember on more than one occasion I cried myself to sleep absolutely from the pang of hunger.*

---

[62] Thompson, Thomas Clarkson, *The Narratives of Thomas Clarkson Thompson, 1860-1938*, edited and annotated by Hugh Thompson Harrington, Gainesville, GA, privately printed, 2019. Available for download online at archive.org and for sale at Amazon.com.

[63] His 13-month journey from Columbia with the slave, William DeSaussure, would bring him back to the family in March 1866. In September 1866, he turned six years old.

On my eighth birthday [September 21, 1868] *Uncle John Thompson* [John Means Thompson, 1842-1882] *sent me fifty cents. Father and mother with their six children* [the author believes there were 5 living children in 1868] *had spent the summer on the farm of Uncle John Clarkson* [John Ouldfield Clarkson, 1837-1895] *a few miles from Columbia. There we lived scantily on corn pone and vegetables during the summer months. We returned to Columbia on September 21ˢᵗ so that Father could get his school rooms ready for the Fall session. As soon as we reached Columbia late in the afternoon, I went to the grocery store and bought a can of sardines, a piece of cheese and some crackers. The five children went to bed, after a supper of a pone of cold corn bread and a small apple. When I produced my supply of good things, Father wanted to wake the other children up to share it with us, but Mother insisted that it was not enough to go around. We sat there in the dining room of the old Male Academy Building and partook of our wonderful birthday party. We then discussed the situation. Mother had some cold mush that she had brought from the farm and a small jug of black sorghum which was to be our breakfast. How my mother kept her family together and kept us from starving I have never been able to figure out, but she did it, kept my father boosted all the time, never lost heart, always cheerful, and saw everything from the bright side. A wonderful woman. My father went far but much of his success in life was due to my mother.*

It was about this time that my mother pawned her wedding ring to get bread for her children. I never knew this until many years after and I don't think that my father ever knew it. Of course, her ring was never regained.[64]

---

[64] Thompson, T. C., *The Narratives of Thomas Clarkson Thompson, 1860-1938*, edited and annotated by H. T. Harrington, 1-13. Available at Amazon.com and archive.org.

Being Principal of the Columbia Male Academy may sound like a well-paying position. It wasn't. Times were tough for the Thompsons as well as the parents of the students. The Thompsons suffered and scraped along for years. Hugh Thompson continually placed advertisements in the newspapers seeking students to enable the struggling school to survive.

In May of 1873, Washington and Lee University, also struggling to stay alive, was raising funds from the southern states through subscriptions for the endowment of academic chairs. Several states had already contributed the $50,000 required for a chair. Hugh S. Thompson contributed $250, which entitled him to a "certificate of scholarship" as well as four coupons which could be redeemed for four years of tuition and college fees.[65] It is not known who benefitted from his coupons.

In 1866, General Thomas H. Ruger, the military Governor of South Carolina, ordered that the graves of the Confederate soldiers were not to be decorated with flowers on April 26th, now known as Confederate Memorial Day. To avoid this order, Leize Thompson and other ladies decorated the graves at night. There were no repercussions.[66] Leize was a champion of Confederate veterans throughout her life.

The Thompsons welcomed the birth of another son, Waddy Thompson[67] on August 13, 1867. He, of course, was a mixed blessing as he was yet another mouth to feed.

On October 6, 1867, the famous "poet laureate of the Confederacy" Henry Timrod died. He and Hugh had been friends. Timrod had been ill for several years, and Hugh was with him almost every day the final week of his life and sat with

---

[65] *The Daily Phoenix* (Columbia, SC), May 18, 1873.
[66] Thompson, T.C., *The Narratives of Thomas Clarkson Thompson, 1860-1938*, edited and annotated by H. T. Harrington, 23. Available at Amazon.com and archive.org.
[67] Waddy Thompson (1867-1939), graduated from the University of South Carolina in 1887, Phi Beta Kappa. He was a historian, newspaperman.

him on his last night.[68] Hugh organized a subscription among friends which bought the tombstone for Timrod, who was buried in the churchyard of Trinity Church. That tombstone has since been replaced with another, more elaborate, stone.

The Thompsons welcomed two more children in 1872. Hugh Smith Thompson[69] was born on January 19 and Elizabeth Clarkson Thompson[70] on December 5th. She would be known as "Elise" in the family.

The Thompson's last child, Caroline Beaumont Thompson,[71] was born June 10, 1874, during the period of tumultuous political unrest in South Carolina. She was their 13th child.

---

[68] Henry Tazewell Thompson, 1859-1932, a son of HST, authored *Henry Timrod, Laureate of the Confederacy*, Columbia: The State Company, 1928.

[69] Hugh S. Thompson (1872-1917) was a real estate broker in New York City.

[70] Elizabeth "Elize" Clarkson Thompson (1872-1942), married lawyer and broker, James Greer Zachry. They lived in New York City.

[71] Caroline Beaumont Thompson (1874-1969) married John Madison Harrington (1874-1925). She was named for her aunt, Caroline Beaumont Clarkson (1834-1912), wife of Lemuel C. Clarke (1831-1893).

Chapter 4
Election of 1876
Wade Hampton, Governor, and Hugh S. Thompson, State Superintendent of Education

After the Civil War, the South, and particularly South Carolina, went through great social, political, and economic turbulence. This turbulence brought about enormous changes. In the simplest terms, the white plantation class had been removed from its former position of privilege in commerce and politics. Hugh and his wife were of this class. Their son, Thomas Clarkson Thompson, wrote about some of what he witnessed. Those observations are collected in the book, *The Narratives of Thomas Clarkson Thompson.*[72]

Carpetbaggers, those men from the North who came south to exploit the political, racial, and economic turmoil, aligned themselves with the former slaves in the first years of the slaves' freedom. These opportunists were not seeking to help the Black people of South Carolina but rather to benefit themselves through financial gain and political power. Scalawags, the same sort of people but from the South, had similar goals.[73]

---

[72] Thompson, T.C., *The Narratives of Thomas Clarkson Thompson, 1860-1938,* edited and annotated by H. T. Harrington. Available at Amazon.com and archive.org.

[73] Thompson, Henry Tazewell (1859-1932), son of Hugh S. Thompson, *Ousting the Carpetbagger from South Carolina* (Columbia, SC: The R.L. Bryan Company, 1927). This book tells the story of this period from an educated Southerner's point of view. Large parts of the book make for uncomfortable reading to the modern eye. However, read with the understanding that the culture was very different in the second half of the 19th century than it is in the first half of the 21st century, the book conveys a great deal of history and explanation of the viewpoint of the white southerner of the period. Henry T. Thompson dedicated his book to "The

Between 1868 and 1875, the Republican party, consisting almost entirely of freed Blacks, scalawags and carpetbaggers, completely controlled the legislature of South Carolina to the exclusion of whites. Civil rights acts were passed

> *to enforce equal rights for both races in matters of public accommodation and entertainment, as on railroads and in hotels, restaurants and theatres. The white people of the State were willing to acquiesce in the political and civil rights granted by the amendments to the U.S. Constitution, but were unwilling to allow them, and never did allow them, entirely, equal social rights, even in cases required by State laws.*[74]

The 1876 political question boiled down to which race should rule the other. It was simply race against race; white against Black.[75]

The overwhelmingly Black policing authorities of the national, state and municipal governments sided with the Black population against the whites. It became clear to the whites that they would have to rely, for their self-defense, on an armed volunteer force of their own. The white solution was the organization of rifle clubs.

The rifle clubs declared in their constitutions that they were created for the promotion of "social intercourse and the enjoyment of its members by means of target shooting…" The clubs, generally, bought their own arms and equipment. Military organizations, not part of the all Black state militia, were prohibited by law. Unquestionably, the rifle clubs were paramilitary organizations. The officers of these extra-legal

---

Red Shirts of 1876, in every walk of life, to whose unceasing vigilance, tireless energy and exalted patriotism, was due the overthrow of Republican misrule and the Ousting of the Carpetbagger from South Carolina."

Another useful book of the period is Williams, Alfred B., *Hampton and His Red Shirts, South Carolina's Deliverance in 1876*, (Charleston, SC: Walker, Evans & Cogswell Company, 1935). Much of it makes uncomfortable reading to the modern eye.

[74] Thompson, Henry T., *Ousting the Carpetbagger*, 68.

[75] Wallace, David Duncan, *South Carolina, A Short History 1520-1948*, Columbia: University of South Carolina Press, 1951, 599.

white militias, the rifle clubs, therefore did not carry military titles. The captain was known as the President; lieutenants as Vice Presidents; sergeants as Wardens; and corporals as Directors. They held shooting matches, parades, dinners, and dances, as well as provided honor guards for events at Confederate cemeteries and other social functions.

The real object of the rifle clubs, however, was the protection of their homes and families in the event of civil unrest, as the white population largely did not believe the Black state militia would provide security.[76] In addition, the rifle clubs would provide assistance, in various forms, to Democrat politicians. About 290 rifle clubs sprang up throughout the state.[77]

It should be pointed out that during the 19th century target shooting was a popular sport in the United States. Often huge crowds numbering into the thousands would attend rifle matches. The most famous of these matches was held on Long Island, New York at a facility known as Creedmore, 15 miles east of New York City. The firing line was 570 feet wide and the range was 1,200 yards long. The Long Island Railroad put in a station at Creedmore to handle the large number of spectators.[78] Unlike the clubs in South Carolina, these shooting clubs had no policing, security or political functions.

Henry Tazewell Thompson wrote in his *The Establishment of the Public School System of South Carolina* that, "In 1874 Captain Thompson was elected president of the Richland Rifle Club, which, as a semi-social and military organization, played an important part in the stirring episodes of Reconstruction and the campaign of 1876."[79] It is uncertain just what, precisely, Hugh Thompson's role was. Apparently, the rifle clubs left no written records regarding political or militia type activities.

---

[76] Thompson, Henry T., *Ousting the Carpetbagger*, 71.

[77] Wallace, David Duncan, *South Carolina, A Short History 1520-1948*, Columbia: University of South Carolina Press, 1951, 601.

[78] Harrington, Hugh T., *More Milledgeville Memories* (Charleston, SC: The History Press, 2006), 63.

[79] Thompson, Henry T., *The Establishment of the Public School System of South Carolina* (Columbia, SC: The R.L. Bryan Company, 1927), 54.

On October 5th, 1874, a near riot took place in Columbia between rival factions supporting Beverly Nash and Charles Minort, both Black Republican candidates for the State Senate from Richland County. In response, a Black militia regiment, in uniform and under arms, under colonel Charles Minort was called out. The regiment was no help but rather sided with those who supported the candidacy of Minort. Huge crowds swarmed the streets. The militia went to the residence of the white Republican Governor Franklin J. Moses, which unnerved the scalawag Governor. He contacted the Richland Rifle Club asking for assistance in preserving the peace.

As President of the Richland Rifle Club, Hugh S. Thompson replied:

October 5, 1874

To his Excellency, F.J. Moses, Jr.,
Governor of South Carolina

Sir:

In response to your application made this afternoon to some of the officers of the Richland Rifle Club to obey an order of your Excellency to be ready as a posse comitatus to preserve the peace in case of a riot between the Minort and the Nash factions which your Excellency apprehends may occur tonight, as President of the Club, and after full consultation with its officers, I have the honor to inform you that the members of the Club are ready to discharge their duty as good citizens and that they will promptly obey any written order to conserve the peace that your Excellency may extend.

Very respectfully,
Your o'b't serv't,
Hugh S. Thompson
President

Henry T. Thompson, Hugh's son, wrote that, "In an almost incredibly short time seventy well-disciplined and well drilled white soldiers, members of the Richland Rifle Club, had assembled. The knowledge that the rifle club was under arms had a wholesome effect upon the riotous men. Governor Moses particularly thanked the Richland Rifle Club after quiet had been restored."[80]

The Daily Phoenix, a Columbia South Carolina newspaper, carried an article on October 22, 1874, stating:

> *The Richland Rifle Club, President Hugh S. Thompson, Esq., were out Tuesday evening in full force, for company drill, on the green adjoining the Columbia Male Academy. They wore, for the first time, their new and beautiful uniform, of historic gray, and went through the maneuvers and evolutions with a gratifying success, encouraged by the presence of a large number of spectators, including many ladies. In a short time, a handsome flag will be presented to the company by some of their fair friends, the reception of which they will honor by a public parade.[81]*

Uniformed armed men drilling on the green would certainly give an unspoken message of the possibility of violence and intimidation.

On February 4, 1875, the Richland Rifle Club held a ball. The newspaper wrote, "The Rifles are a fine body of men, under the leadership of Capt. Hugh S. Thompson. The company numbers 107, and yet the organization is scarcely six months old."[82] Officially the officers of the Rifle Clubs did not bear military titles. Hugh Thompson, however, was commonly referred to in public as "Captain" as that was his title during the Civil War. His title with the rifle club was President.

The Richland Rifle Club eventually evolved into the Governor's Guards, which won first place in the interstate drill held at the Fair Grounds in Columbia in 1877. In 1878 it reorganized as the Richland Battalion, and Hugh commanded it. In 1881 he was elected Colonel of the Palmetto Regiment, which he led at the Yorktown battle centennial.[83] However, prior to

---

[80] Thompson, Henry T., *Ousting the Carpetbagger*, 72-73.
[81] *The Daily Phoenix* (Columbia, SC), October 22, 1874.
[82] *The Daily Phoenix* (Columbia, SC), February 2, 1875.
[83] Thompson, Henry T., *The Establishment of the Public School System*, 55.

the 1876 election, the Richland Rifle Club was an active political tool. Some may say it was a weapon, a sharp-edged weapon.

From 1865 through 1880, Hugh was principal of the Columbia Male Academy on Laurel Street in Columbia. He was a professional educator; his military service with The Citadel cadets had been by necessity rather than profession. Since the founding of South Carolina until the Civil War, the well-to-do sent their children to private schools or hired tutors for their sons and governesses for their daughters.[84]

Private academies, such as the Columbia Male Academy, were common in each county. Some were co-educational. Girls often went to seminaries for their education. The principals of the academies were usually men of considerable scholarship and literary abilities. Mathematics and the classics were emphasized.

Many, if not most, parents at that time considered the education of their children part of the responsibility of parentage, not the role of the public sector. The first state-supported free schools began in South Carolina in 1811. The goal was to provide "elementary instruction to be imparted to all pupils free of charge, preference being given to poor orphans and children of indigent parents." There was a stigma of poverty attached to the free schools that kept all but the poor from attending. There were no arrangements for the education of Black students. The tax-paying public largely objected to paying taxes for the schools, believing that education was the duty of the parents, not the state.[85]

The resulting situation arose where the wealthy were not sending their children to the free schools as they did not need them, and the poor whites were not sending their children to the free schools as they did not want to be branded as paupers. Therefore, poor white children did not get an education.

---

[84] Thompson, Henry T., *The Establishment of the Public School System*, 3.
[85] Thompson, Henry T., *The Establishment of the Public School System*, 5-7.

With the advent of Reconstruction and the 1868 South Carolina Constitution, free schools, colleges and universities were established. Whites were reluctant to go to schools taught by northern teachers and would not attend schools that accepted Blacks. They also were adamantly against equality of teaching Blacks as well as whites, even in separate schools.[86]

State politics and civil unrest not only continued but became increasingly violent. Racial strife was rampant. Republican Governor Moses was not reelected in 1874, with the governorship going to the Republican Daniel H. Chamberlain. Daniel H. Chamberlain was a white Republican and a member of the party of Lincoln. He was born in Massachusetts and had served in the Union army. He was considered a carpetbagger.

Without going deeply into the heated politics, it can be said, although over simplified, that the white population was greatly disturbed by the Republican rule and by the overwhelming domination of state government by Blacks who outnumbered the whites in most South Carolina counties. The aim of the Democrats was a return to rule by the white minority.

In May 1875, the Richland Rifle Club held a picnic. Prior to the social events the "well-disciplined and well-drilled corps assembled...armed and equipped for a target match." They marched to the target field in their "uniforms of venerated grey," preceded by the "excellent band of the 18th United States Infantry" that was stationed at Columbia as part of the occupying force. The Rifle Club's drilling paid off as, under the command of Captain Thompson, "they moved off as one man. Their soldierly tread, precision of movement, perfect performance of evolutions and promptness of obedience to command were highly credible to the ability of the officers, as well as to the price and application of the entire club." A huge crowd of well-wishers, including the wives, girlfriends and admiring young ladies, was in attendance.

The target shooting was one of the highlights of the day, and a good time was had by all. Several of the riflemen were

---

[86] Thompson, Henry T., *The Establishment of the Public School System*, 10-15.

excellent marksmen. Others were not. The prize to the best shooter was awarded, along with a short speech, by probably the only Republican present, South Carolina Governor Daniel H. Chamberlain. Eleven shooters failed to hit the target with any of their shots. They chose lots among themselves and the lucky loser was T. Simons Clarkson,[87] who was awarded a tin cup to great applause and the delight of the assembled crowd. The officers held a match separately. The winner, perhaps displaying skills learned at The Citadel, was Hugh S. Thompson.[88]

The year 1876 was an election year with the election being held in November. In August, the Democrats nominated former Confederate General Wade Hampton III for governor. He was widely and enthusiastically endorsed by the vast majority of white people. Others on the ticket were W.D. Simpson for Lt. Governor, R.M. Sims for Secretary of State, General James Conner for Attorney General, General Johnson Hagood for Comptroller-General, S.C. Leaphart for Treasurer, and E.W. Moise for Adjutant General. Hugh S. Thompson was nominated for State Superintendent of Education.

Clearly, Hampton was a white supremacist and proponent of what is known in the 21st century as the "Lost Cause." He was believed to be the only candidate that could unite the Democrats. The white Democrats had a tough problem. Blacks outnumbered the whites three to two, potentially outvoting the Democrats by 30,000. A fair election simply could not be won by white voters. The Democrats knew, if they were to win, extraordinary measures were called for.

In September the Republicans nominated Daniel H. Chamberlain, the current governor. The stage was set for a battle for control, and the future, of South Carolina. The campaign would be furious and very dirty. He was backed almost entirely by Blacks as well as scalawag and carpetbagger opportunists. Racism was the primary issue. The Republican

---

[87] Thomas Simons Clarkson (1854-1904) was the nephew of Hugh S. Thompson's wife, Elizabeth Clarkson Thompson.
[88] *The Daily Phoenix* (Columbia, SC), May 6, 1875.

state government had been run without white representation or participation. The Democrat white population was determined to regain their pre-Reconstruction positions of authority.

When Hampton and the other Democratic candidates, including Thompson appeared, as they did in every county, crowds of whites would gather to see Hampton, their Civil War hero, and cheer the speakers. Rifle clubs would be there along with the Red Shirt companies, which had evolved from a grass-roots movement to elect Wade Hampton and take back control of the government.

As the name implies, the Red Shirt companies consisted of red-shirted Democrat volunteers from across the state, armed and mounted on horseback. They used intimidation and violence to reach their objectives. The Red Shirts were a paramilitary organization that in the 21st century would be seen by most as a dangerous extremist, radical militia organization. Masses of Democrats, along with non-voting white women, would turn out for political rallies with the great hope that Election Day, November 7th, would remove the existing Republican government.

A typical campaigning day would include bands playing, parading rifle clubs and Red Shirts on horseback, patriotic decorations, wild cheering, singing of "We'll hang Dan Chamberlain on a sour apple tree," food, the rebel yell, drink, and great enthusiasm. It was a massive outdoor social event for thousands of men and women featuring far more than mere speeches from the candidates. In many ways it was a spectacle much like a huge carnival. "Hurrah for Hampton" was the slogan on the lips of countless white people.

The enforcement, or strong-arm, activities were in the hands of the rifle clubs and the Red Shirts. While extreme violence was to be avoided, if possible, much violence did often take place. To influence the Republican majority three methods were utilized. Simple persuasion was the first but not often successful. Inducing Republicans not to go to the polls was another tactic. This included instilling the fear of loss of employment should they vote. However, the most effective method was intimidation. This intimidation was not always violent, but the threat of violence was real. If, unexpectedly, mounted Red Shirts should appear on the streets of a town either silently or firing pistols into the air, the message was clear to stay away from the polls. Red Shirts would also break up Republican political meetings and shout down Republican speakers. Intimidation worked both ways as Republican groups would threaten white voters, as well. However, the Democrats were better, more effective, at intimidation.

At that time, the Ku Klux Klan (KKK) had been the target of various Federal laws designed to suppress, even crush, its violent and intimidating tactics. The KKK therefore was not involved, as an organization, in the current elections. However, the men who had been members in the KKK still existed as individuals. Some, perhaps many or most, of those men were now members of the rifle clubs or Red Shirts. Meanwhile there is no evidence that Hugh Thompson was involved in the vestiges of the KKK or supported the KKK. In the 1890s, his son, Thomas Clarkson Thompson, would fight against the KKK in Dalton, Georgia.[89]

However, the KKK's methods and goals somewhat overlapped with that of the rifle clubs and Red Shirts. One distinction was that while the KKK was a secret organization, the rifle clubs and Red Shirts did not cover their faces and were not concerned that their identities were known. All three organizations may have been considered in the 21st century as terrorist groups. However, in the 19th century, they were not considered so, at least by the white population.

A witness described one method used by the Red Shirts:

Clubs of irresponsible young men, mounted and uniformed with the Red Shirt, are summoned, paraded, and maneuvered...The streets and roads leading to the place of meetings are seized upon by these mounted bodies, and timid and responsible citizens are...deterred from attending their meetings by the clamor, the

---

[89] Thompson, Thomas Clarkson, *The Narratives of Thomas Clarkson Thompson, 1860-1938,* edited and annotated by Hugh Thompson Harrington, Gainesville, GA, privately printed, 2019. Available for download online at archive.org and for sale at Amazon.com.

galloping of horses, and the yell of men, mingled with the reckless discharge of firearms.[90]

White women of South Carolina encouraged their men enthusiastically. They fed Red Shirt Democrats passing their homes, considering them patriots. Red was a popular color in clothing, signifying support for the Red Shirts. Women would wear red ribbons in their hair as a sign of their support. In rural areas in particular, the threat of negro uprisings, whether valid or not, added to the tension.[91]

While there is no evidence that he was a member, Hugh Smith Thompson (and Elizabeth Clarkson Thompson) likely supported the Red Shirts because the Red Shirts supported the Democratic ticket, of which he was a part. Lieze Thompson is known to have been a very strong and supportive woman. It is certain she backed up whatever Hugh was doing, but unfortunately the details of their precise activities are unknown. However, Hugh's leadership in the rifle clubs is well documented.

On October 7th at Sumter, South Carolina, Hampton was about to give a campaign speech. As he walked to the speakers' stand a

> *bowed figure draped in robes of dense black and wrapped with chains stepped to the platform above and before him. As he ascended the chains were cast aside with a clang, the mourning robes were thrown off and a radiant young woman in pure white stood tall and stately, head up-lifted and eyes shining like stars with*

---

[90] Barnes, Brooks Miles, "Southern Independents: South Carolina, 1882," *The South Carolina Historical Magazine*, July 1995, vol. 96, No. 3, pp. 230-251.

[91] Much of the material regarding the campaign tactics of 1876 comes from Thompson, Henry T., *The Establishment of the Public School System*, 112-119. A far more comprehensive view, from the Southern perspective, is found in Williams, Alfred B., *Hampton and His Red Shirts*.

*excitement and pleasure, a golden coronet on her hair –
"South Carolina."*[92]

Such emotional theater, sometimes accompanied by cannon fire, was common.

On the 7th of October, Governor D.H. Chamberlain issued a proclamation requiring the rifle clubs to disband. This proclamation was received with an uproar from the Democratic newspapers. The *Pickens Sentinel* of Pickens, South Carolina reported that "the sham reformer and bald headed fraud, D.H. Chamberlain, has issued a proclamation, disbanding all the Rifle Clubs in the State, commanding them to 'disperse and retire peaceably to their homes,' as though a terrible rebellion was on hand. There was never a more peaceable or quiet campaign in this State, and the fraud knows it. But like all other drowning men he catches at straws."[93] The article continues in this vein.

Other, less hysterical, newspapers suggested thoughts such as the Governor "places a large and respectable number of the citizens of this State in the position of an armed mob." Also, many of the men of the rifle clubs owned their rifles as individuals, and the second amendment to the Constitution granted them that right. In addition, it was pointed out that citizens are permitted by the Constitution to assemble and attend public meetings. Their right to do so while carrying banners and shouting "huzzah for the candidates of their choice" ought not to be "wiped out by the mere stroke of a gubernatorial pen."[94]

President Ulysses S. Grant issued his own proclamation on October 17, 1876. He stated, in part:

---

[92] Williams, Alfred B., *Hampton and His Red Shirts, South Carolina's Deliverance in 1876*, Charleston: Walker, Evans & Cogswell Company, 1935, p. 245. Wallace, David Duncan, *South Carolina a Short History*, Columbia: University of SC Press, 1951, p. 601. Wallace locates this event as Abbeville, Williams has it as Sumter; perhaps it was a feature at both.
[93] "The Proclamation," *The Pickens Sentinel* (Pickens, SC) October 12, 1876.
[94] "Latest Wave of the Bloody Shirt," *Yorkville Enquirer* (York, SC) October 12, 1876.

Whereas It has been satisfactorily shown to me that insurrection and domestic violence exist in several counties of the State of South Carolina, and that certain combinations of men against law exist in many counties of said State known as "rifle clubs," who ride up and down, by day and night, in arms, murdering some peaceable citizens and intimidating others, which combinations, though forbidden by the laws of the State cannot be controlled or suppressed by the ordinary course of justice...

Grant cited his duty, when called upon by the Governor, to supply U.S. military forces "as may be necessary and adequate to protect said State and the citizens thereof against domestic violence..." He issued his proclamation commanding "all persons engaged in said unlawful and insurrectionary proceedings to disperse and retire peaceably..."[95]

The New York City newspaper *The New York Daily Herald* under the headline "Ballots and Bullets, Thirty Two Companies of Troops in South Carolina, Governor Chamberlain's Letter to the Richland Rifle Club" described how the presence of the 1600 Federal troops in South Carolina would "result in undoing the disintegration effected among the negroes by the whites, and cause a consolidation of that vote for the Republican candidates." In other words, the presence of the troops would encourage, embolden and bring out the Black vote for the Republican candidates. The paper opined that the Democrats hope, "to carry the State for Hampton by a decisive majority, if a fair count and fair election is allowed by Chamberlain and his candidates, who constitute the Commissioners of Election and State Board of Canvassers."

Governor Chamberlain wrote Hugh S. Thompson formally on October 21, 1876, addressing him as "Captain, Richland Rifle Club, Columbia, SC.":

---

[95] "Proclamation by the President," *The Intelligencer* (Anderson, SC) October 26, 1876.

Sir,

On August 18, 1874, as appears by the record of the Adjutant General's office, you received from the State forty-five Remington rifles, with equipment for the use of the Richland Rifle Club, I am now compelled by my official duty to direct that the above named arms be forthwith delivered to James Kennedy, Esq. at the Armory of the state militia in this city. I further request to be informed by you whether the Richland Rifle Club still exists as an organization or not, and I refer you to my proclamation of the 7th inst. and that of the President of the United States of the 17th inst.

Very respectfully, D.H. Chamberlain,
Governor of South Carolina

Hugh Thompson replied on October 23, 1876:

Sir,

In reply to your communication of the 21st inst., directing the return forthwith to James Kennedy, Esq., of forty-five Remington rifles, issued August 18, 1874, to the Richland Rifle Club, I have to state that the arms are now in the hands of the gentlemen formerly composing the club. The club having been disbanded, I will use all possible personal diligence in collecting the arms and returning them as directed.

Very respectfully, Hugh S. Thompson

The New York Daily Herald, described Hugh Thompson's response as "The Governor Checkmated," reporting that *during the present campaign this club had merely continued its ordinary drills and meetings and had made no demonstration, that could in the least have shocked the delicate nerves and tender sensibilities of the Governor. On the issuing of the proclamation, the club disbanded. The Governor's letter was evidently intended to provoke a disturbance. A bond had been filed conditioned for the return of the guns after the expiration of a specified period upon demand made, and his hope doubtless was that the club would refuse to return the arms, preferring to forfeit the bond, and that he would thereby have a pretext for ordering federal troops to disarm them. Mr. Thompson has, however, on the contrary, by his response, disarmed the Governor, and wipes out the anticipated speck of war.*

The newspaper pointed out that

Governor Chamberlain has partaken of the hospitality of the club, distributed prizes at target shootings and suggested the formation of a rifle team from its members to compete at the Centennial. He marched in procession with it at the Fort Moultrie Centennial, and in a short address before it alluded with pride to the citizen soldiers of the State. No more conclusive proof of the farcical aspect of the military occupation [of Columbia and the State of South Carolina] *can be furnished than that 5,000 rounds of ammunition were issued to a company of twenty-three rank and file and to the other commands in proportion.*[96]

James Conner, the candidate for Attorney General, wrote to his wife October 24th that

the Rifle Clubs are disbanded. We found ourselves so hampered we could not work the organization, and we broke up the armories, distributed the arms among the men, and will, in case of need, assemble as individuals at certain fixed rendezvous in each ward. It really makes the force more effective. Some of the younger men – particularly among the Carolinas, are very much dissatisfied. They do not consider it except in the light of their own wishes – but it was necessary and was urged

---

[96] *The New York Daily Herald* (New York), October 24, 1876, p. 7.

The response to the President's proclamation from the Democratic party's Executive Committee was swift. The Democratic position was that Grant was reacting to the statements made by Governor Chamberlain "which are aimed exclusively against his political opponents...that every resident knows them to be untrue." In addition, "every Republican of character or intelligence, or who is not in office or seeking office, and many who are in office in the State, have expressed horror and disgust at the course which the Governor has pursued."

The Democratic party's Executive Committee stated that "we bow in perfect submission to the proclamation of his Excellency the President, and exhort our fellow-citizens whom we represent in the present canvass to yield full and entire obedience to every command of the said proclamation." Further, "we repeat that we speak without disrespect to the President of the United States. He acts upon the statements made by the Governor of this State. But we say it that we may show our unwillingness to obey without committing an untruth against ourselves by seeming to acknowledge that of which we are not guilty."[98]

In other words, the Democrats would do as the President of the United States ordered, but in doing so they are not acknowledging that what they, as Democrats, have done or intended on doing was in any way wrong or illegal.

It is no surprise that the election was fraught with massive fraud by both the Democrats and the Republicans. It is fortunate we have a firsthand account written over a half century later by Hugh's then 18-year-old son, Thomas Clarkson Thompson, of his own activities during the 1876 or 1878 election. He is not

---

[97] Moffett, Mary Conner, *Letters of General James Conner, C.S.A.*, Columbia: The R.L. Bryan Co., 1950, 221.
[98] "Address to the People of South Carolina," *The Newberry Weekly Herald* (Newberry, SC) October 25, 1876.

clear about which election he referred to. It can be assumed that the same or similar tactics were used in both.

He wrote,

There were few negroes [who] *voted the democratic ticket on account of General Hampton. The night before this election I spent the night in the office of one of the large cotton firms in Charleston with a dozen other young men rolling the tissue ballots inside the Republican ballot so they might be readily handled the next day at the polls.*

Apparently, this was a method of stuffing the ballot box with fraudulent votes, the exact procedure is unclear.[99]

Thomas Clarkson Thompson also wrote specifically about some 1878 election tactics that likely were also used in 1876. He describes arrangements being made with the superintendent of the railroad repair shops to

put all clocks back and not allow the six o'clock whistle to be blown until some fifteen or twenty minutes late. This was done to prevent the negro employees of the road, some 90%, from getting to the polls in time to vote. About 10 minutes of six a...negro...came in to vote and after giving his name and age as 33 he was asked what year he was born, and he replied '1876.' The Democratic party bodily put him over the fence with the statement that he was only two years old and could not vote.

The explanation of the opportunity to do these things is that the law required that there should be two members only of one party and one member of the other as watchers and counters. In most cases the members of the radical [Republican] *party were negroes and they were either bribed or bull-dozed or made too drunk to take care of their job.*[100]

---

[99] Thompson, Thomas Clarkson, *The Narratives of Thomas Clarkson Thompson, 1860-1938*, edited and annotated by H. T. Harrington, 24.
[100] Thompson, Thomas Clarkson, *The Narratives of Thomas Clarkson Thompson, 1860-1938*, edited and annotated by H. T. Harrington, 24

The election results showed that Wade Hampton had won. Whether he actually did win or not is impossible to say for certain. Fraud accusations were charged by both sides, and both sides claimed victory. The vote was close. The state board of Canvassers, made up of five Republican officials, tallied the result and found that Hampton received 92,261 votes compared to 91,127 for Chamberlain. However, the Board determined that the elections in Edgefield and Laurens counties were severely tainted and arbitrarily excluded those ballots. Their final tabulation changed a 1,134 Republican defeat into a 3,145-vote victory. [101] This, naturally, caused an uproar. Both the Republicans and the Democrats claimed victory.

South Carolina faced the bizarre situation of two parties both claiming to be the "elected" House of Representatives and "elected" Governor, and both parties were determined to carry on the government. Both sets of the legislature passed laws and made statements about the opposing legislature. Chamberlain and Hampton each held inaugurations in December 1876. Chamberlain and Hampton, each believing he was the rightfully elected Governor, signed his correspondence as "Governor of South Carolina." The details of the resolution of this dual governorship are long and complicated.

In 2001 a complex analysis of the 1876 election was undertaken. The result was that the Democrat Hampton received a majority of the votes cast and counted. However, it concludes that "if the voting had been free from violence and fraud the Republican majority would have been sufficiently large to elect all the candidates for state offices."[102]

---

[101] King, Ronald F., "Counting the Votes: South Carolina's Stolen Election of 1876," *Journal of Interdisciplinary History*, vol. 32, No. 2, Autumn 2001, pp. 169-191.
[102] Ibid.

Chapter 5
Post-Election of 1876
It ain't over till it's over

In the Spring of 1877, five months after the election, the difficulties had not been resolved. Backed by Federal troops, Governor Chamberlain still held the Statehouse. There was no functioning government in South Carolina.

President Grant issued orders that the rifle clubs were not to parade on February 22nd in memory of George Washington. *The Weekly Union* (Union, SC) wrote, on March 2, 1877, under the headline, "The Heel of the Dying Tyrant" regarding the orders from President Grant:[103]

When the Potomac boats pass Mt. Vernon even at this late day, when every vestige of republican government and American liberty is gone, they toll a requiem [fire a cannon salute] *to the memory of the immortal Washington; but it remains for the "drunken Galena tanner"* [reference to President Grant] *to forbid freeborn American citizens in South Carolina from an innocent display of their patriotism on the 22nd of February 1877. Last night the gallant Col. Black, a gentleman and a patriot, who fought for 'the old flag'* [a southerner, who fought for the Union], *and who is here among us merely as "a looker on in Vienna,"* [from Shakespeare, "Measure for Measure," Act 5, Scene 1] *in an official way, received orders dictated by the dying dog* [President Grant], *and instigated by the carpet-bag pretender from Massachusetts* [Gov. Chamberlain], *at present in our midst, which compels him to address the following note to Capt. Hugh S. Thompson of the militia.*[104]

---

[103] *The Weekly Union* (Union, SC), March 2, 1877, p. 1.

[104] It is interesting, even fascinating, that *The Weekly Union* newspaper editor, Robert M. Stokes (2/11/1817-12/10/1898), used such language

The note referred to by Lt. Col. H.M. Black, the commander of the 18th US Infantry Post at Columbia, was dated February 20, 1877 and was to Hugh S. Thompson, addressing him as "Captain".

Sir,

I have the honor to notify you that I have this day been directed by the honorable Secretary of War [J. Donald Cameron] to inform you that his Excellency the President of the United States [Ulysses S. Grant] directs me to notify you that the members of the so-called rifle clubs, who, under his proclamation of the 17th of October last, were instructed to disband, will not be permitted to make any demonstration or parade on the 22d instant, as is said to be contemplated; and it is hoped you will give a cheerful obedience to this order, and notify the members of your club, or company, thereof, in order to prevent a parade taking place.

My orders require me to see that no such parade takes place.

I am, sir, very respectfully,
your obedient servant,
H.M. Black,
Lieutenant Colonel 18th Infantry,
Commanding Post[105]

---

toward President Grant as "dying dog," "dying tyrant," and "drunken Galena tanner." Stokes also called Governor Chamberlain a "carpet-bag pretender." Editor Stokes used the phrase "a looker on in Vienna" referring to Col. Black. The "looker on in Vienna" quote in full is Shakespeare's "My business in this state made me a looker-on here in Vienna where I have seen corruption boil and bubble," which fits the Democratic newspaper's view of Col. Black's situation perfectly. Clearly, the editor was a well-educated man who must have believed that his readership was as well-educated as himself and would pick up on the reference and the full quotation without having it spelled out for them. One wonders what percentage of a modern readership would appreciate Mr. Stokes' scholarship.

[105] *The Weekly Union Times* (Union, SC), March 2, 1877.

Colonel Black reported to the Secretary of War that "this paper [the note] was handed to Captain Thompson, who said, "If you will leave this matter with me, I will assure you that no parade will take place. They all recognize me as the commanding or senior officer."[106]

There was more to the orders from Colonel Black to Hugh Thompson than meets the eye. The February 20, 1877 orders from the Secretary of War, J.D. Cameron, to Colonel Black contains an extraordinarily inflammatory instruction: the use of force.

The Secretary of War's order to Col. H.M. Black is as follows:

The President [Grant] *directs that you notify the members of the so-called rifle clubs, who under his proclamation of the 17th of October, were instructed to disband, not to make any public demonstration or parade on the 22nd instant, as is said to be contemplated, and that, if necessary, you compel obedience to your order by force.*[107] [underline emphasis added]

The idea that, in order to prevent a parade in memory of George Washington, force would be used against the armed men of the rifle clubs is astonishing. Potentially, thousands of men could have responded if force was used by the U.S. Army, creating a major conflict. Col. Black may not have shown Hugh Thompson the orders to him from the Secretary of War, but it seems very likely that the threat of force was at least conveyed verbally, especially as the men had known each other for years; so there would be no misunderstanding of the perilous precipice they both were standing upon.

---

[106] McPherson, Edward, LLD, *A Handbook of Politics for 1878 Being a Record of Important Political Action, National and State, from July 15, 1876, to July 1, 1878*, Washington: Solomon & Chapman, 1878, p. 80.
[107] McPherson, Edward, LLD, *A Handbook of Politics for 1878 Being a Record of Important Political Action, National and State, from July 15, 1876, to July 1, 1878*, Washington: Solomon & Chapman, 1878, p. 80.

Wade Hampton, writing as "Governor" issued a proclamation in response to President Grant's order, the same day, February 20, 1877:

> *His Excellency the President of the United States having ordered that the white militia companies of this State should not parade on the 22d instant, to celebrate Washington's birthday; in deference to the office he holds, I hereby call upon these organizations to postpone to some future day this manifestation of their respect to the memory of that illustrious President, whose highest ambition it was as it was his chief glory, to observe the constitution and obey the laws of the country.*
>
> *If the arbitrary commands of a Chief Executive, who has not sought to emulate the virtues of Washington, deprive the citizens of this State of the privilege of joining publicly in paying reverence to that day, so sacred to every American patriot, we can at least show by our obedience to constituted authority, however arbitrarily exercised, that we are not unworthy to be the countrymen of Washington.*[108]

Hugh Thompson's and Wade Hampton's calming statements quelled any public demonstration or parade. So ended the controversy of the rifle clubs' marching on Washington's birthday.

The controversy over who was governor continued. Wade Hampton, acting as Governor, asked white and Black South Carolinians to pay 10 percent of their prior year tax to the Hampton government and to refuse to pay any tax to the Chamberlain government. Overwhelmingly, taxes flowed to the Hampton government.

On March 31, 1877, four months after the contested election, Chamberlain and Hampton travelled to Washington, DC to meet with the newly elected Republican President Rutherford B. Hayes. They both stated their positions to the

---

[108] *The Weekly Union Times* (Union, SC), March 2, 1877.

President. President Hayes, not wanting State elections to depend upon the presence of Federal troops, decided that he would remove the troops, which had been bolstering Chamberlain's claim for the Governorship, from South Carolina on April 10th. The following day Chamberlain resigned. Hampton and the Democrats took over the government of South Carolina.

A huge gala and reception was staged for Governor Wade Hampton upon his return from Washington by train on the afternoon of April 6th. "All the civic associations, fire companies, military clubs and other organizations, both white and colored, are expected to participate" reported a newspaper. Among the officials of the event was "Captain Hugh S. Thompson, Assistant Marshal in charge of the military."[109]

The return to Columbia of the triumphant Governor Wade Hampton was a huge celebration. One newspaper reported,

while there was an abundant display of bunting, of evergreens and of flowers, and the ladies, as usual, arranged everything with taste and beauty, the reception of Governor Hampton was marked by a hearty feeling of "well done, thou good and faithful servant," upon the part of the citizens, which we have never seen equaled.

The executive office and the building in which it is located had been profusely decorated by the ladies assigned for that purpose – Mrs. Hugh S. Thompson [and three others]...being the principal directors in the decorations. [At] precisely 2 o'clock the procession was formed on Richardson Street, Capt. Hugh S. Thompson in charge of the military portion...[110]

Years later, on the evening of November 7, 1890, newsmen asked Hugh Thompson for his thoughts about Wade Hampton. He replied by describing the scene on the streets of Columbia in 1876:

---

[109] "Grand Ovation to Gov. Hampton," *The Intelligencer* (Anderson, SC), April 5, 1877.
[110] "Gov. Hampton's Return! His Reception at Columbia!", *The Weekly Union Times* (Union, SC) April 13, 1877.

He [Hampton] *has done more good for South Carolina than any man in the present generation. His wise counsels in the past, obedience to which wrought out the State's salvation, place our people under an everlasting debt of gratitude.*

I remember a short speech he made once under the most exciting circumstances, that will give you an idea of the wonderful influence he exercised. It was shortly after the eventful campaign of 1876. Hampton had been elected governor, but Chamberlain claimed the office, and backed by State constabulary and United States soldiers, proposed to hold it. Feeling ran high. Men of the coolest temper were stirred as they had not been since the war. The least spark would have caused an explosion.

The day the legislature met there were at least 5,000 armed men in the streets of Columbia, desperate enough to do anything that promised to relieve us from the oppressions of the party in power. The Democrats had carried the legislature, but the representatives of several counties were not allowed to take their seats. It looked as if their exclusion was bound to bring on trouble. Our people were determined to no longer bear a regime that had grown intolerable.

The armed forces collected about the State house ripe for anything when [Wade] *Hampton mounted the steps of the capitol and addressed them as follows:*

'My friends your presence here embarrasses me greatly. Ever since the day I was nominated I have been trying to pour oil on the troubled waters. Go quietly to your homes, obey the laws, and by the eternal I will yet be governor of South Carolina.'

He had no sooner ceased than the crowd scattered. They took him at his word. Soon afterward we installed him into the gubernatorial office out in the open air, on *the street, for the other party still had the Statehouse, but on the 3rd of May they completely collapsed, and Hampton entered on the first honest and efficient administration we had enjoyed since reconstruction.*[111]

[111] "Hampton and South Carolina," *The Washington Post* (Washington, DC), November 8, 1890, 2.

Chapter 6
State Superintendent of Education

The state officers, including Hugh S. Thompson, now the State Superintendent of Education, did not take their offices until May 1, 1877. The entire work force of the Department of Education in 1877 consisted of Thompson as the State Superintendent of Education and his clerk, Charles M. Tew.[112] Until 1880 Hugh would also continue his duties at the Columbia Male Academy.

Unfortunately, at that time, the Department of Education was in chaos. Corruption and incompetence were rampant. There was a $325,000 deficit, much of which apparently was fraudulent. Also, many teachers had not been paid in months. A continual problem was the idea that education was a private matter and for the State to undertake to educate children was a usurping of parental rights. Also, some believed that education was not necessarily conducive to good citizenship.

Thompson wrote in his annual report for 1882, "the need for trained teachers becomes more apparent as our public school system develops. Teaching is both a science and an art. No science is more progressive; none demands more careful preparation by those who would pursue it successfully."[113]

He overhauled the education of the state in many ways including creating institutes to teach teachers, with separate institutes for Black and white teachers. He was adamant that trained, professional, teachers were essential to a successful public school system.

He received some criticism for creating the public school system for all student populations, to which he responded, "the cause of popular education can suffer no detriment from free,

---

[112] Thompson, Henry T., *The Establishment of the Public School System.* 16-17.

[113] Thompson, Henry T., *The Establishment of the Public School System.* 32.

fair and open discussion. Agitation is a more healthful sign than apathy."[114]

In his 1878 Annual Report he wrote, "One of the greatest dangers will be found in the ignorance of a large number of our people. The returns of the last census show that nearly 57 per cent of the voting population of the State are unable to read the ballots which they cast. No other State in the Union contains so large a proportion of illiterate voters."[115]

In 1879 he wrote, "What this state needs is a system of public schools that will reach down to the lowest classes of society and raise them up; that will elevate the humblest by giving them the virtue and intelligence for which, without State aid, they will never seek."[116]

In light of the extreme racism of the 1876 election, it is of interest to read what Hugh Thompson wrote, in 1879, about educating the Blacks of South Carolina:

...the pledges given in 1876 to secure to the negroes equal educational facilities with the whites have been faithfully kept. ... The rights of citizenship were conferred upon the negroes when they were notoriously unfit to exercise them. How far they, as a class, will prove themselves worthy of all the privileges of citizens, is a question which further experience will be required to determine. It is certain that they cannot be fitted to discharge the duties of free men without education. The white people of South Carolina are contributing liberally of their taxes to the education of the negroes. Fortunate will it be if those outside of the State who continue to agitate the race question shall be induced to show their faith by their works and unite with the white people of South Carolina in giving the negroes the benefit of education. True philanthropy and sound statesmanship

---

[114] Thompson, Henry T., *The Establishment of the Public School System.* p. 40, citing Hugh S. Thompson's 1881 Annual Report, p. 8.

[115] Thompson, Henry T., *The Establishment of the Public School System.* p. 49, citing 1878 report p. 25-26.

[116] Thompson, Henry T., *The Establishment of the Public School System.* p. 50, citing 1879 Annual Report, p. 28.

In February 1882, Hugh Thompson accompanied the Reverend A.D. Mayo, D.D., of Boston, associate editor of the *National Journal of Education*, on a tour of South Carolina. Dr. Mayo was giving a series of lectures on popular education and education in New England. In March, both Hugh Thompson and Dr. Mayo attended the Department of Superintendence of the National Educational Association in Washington, DC.[118]

During 1882, which was Hugh Thompson's last year as State Superintendent of Education, South Carolina College, now the University of South Carolina, which had been partially opened in 1880, was reorganized and fully opened. Also, The Citadel, The Military College of South Carolina, which had closed during the Civil War, was reopened in September 1882.[119]

As speaker at the commencement exercises at Adger College in Walhalla, South Carolina in June 1882, Hugh Thompson addressed the need for the education of the Black race, which was lagging behind that of the white. The races, standing on unequal ground, both needed to be educated to lift themselves for the benefit of all. He stated that while property could be inherited, knowledge could only be acquired. It could not be transmitted from father to son. The knowledge of one generation could be preserved through books, but it could only be acquired by the individual through study. Education must come through the schools. He pointed out that New England, the West and Southwest were preparing their citizens for the highest order of education. Harvard and Yale each had about 1,000 students; the University of Michigan had about 1,200. He

---

[117] Thompson, Henry T., *The Establishment of the Public School System*. p. 52-53, citing 1879 Annual Report, p. 7-11.

[118] *The Intelligencer* (Anderson, SC), February 16, 1882, p. 2 and *The Critic and Record* (Washington, DC), March 22, 18882, p. 3.

[119] Thompson, Henry T., *The Establishment of the Public School System*. p. 40-41.

urged that "if we hope to keep our past prestige in statesmen and scholars, we must move forward in the same direction."[120] He was a progressive for his time and especially in the South.

During the six years that he was head of the Education Department, the number of schools had increased from 2,483 to 3,183 and the number of teachers from 2,674 to 3,413. Attendance increased from 102,396 to 145,974.

In recognition of his work as state superintendent, the current South Carolina Department of Education proclaims, "Hugh S. Thompson is known as the father of South Carolina's modern public school system."[121]

---

[120] *Keowee Courier* (Pickens, SC) Jun3 29, 1882, p. 1.
[121] South Carolina Department of Education, https://ed.sc.gov/newsroom/former-state-superintendents-of-education/hugh-s-thompson/ accessed May 3, 2024.

Chapter 7

1882: Governor of South Carolina

In addition to his work in the Education Department, Hugh Thompson was involved in other activities. He was active in the revitalization of South Carolina's Palmetto Regiment in 1881. He was elected Colonel, a position he held until his resignation in March 1883. This unit participated in various Revolutionary War centennial events such as Cowpens and Yorktown.[122]

Hugh Smith Thompson, Colonel of the Palmetto Regt, 1881

Just prior to the expiration of his last term as State Superintendent of Education, Hugh was offered the superintendency of The Citadel, which he declined. He was also offered the presidency of South Carolina College, now The University of South Carolina, which he provisionally accepted.

Before he could assume the presidency, the Democratic Convention of 1882 nominated him for Governor. The

---

[122] *Yorkville Enquirer* (York, SC), May 19, 1881. *Norfolk Landmark* (Norfolk, VA), April 26, 1881, *Richmond Dispatch* (Richmond, VA), June 30, 1881.

nomination came as a surprise as he was not a candidate and had not sought to be a candidate. The Convention was deadlocked over two candidates. Hugh S. Thompson, a compromise candidate, was chosen as a man that all would accept.[123] He was 46 years old.

After his nomination for Governor, he addressed the Convention saying,

> *It is but simple truth for me to say that the honor you have conferred upon me is one which I neither solicited, expected nor desired. It would be less than the truth if I did not express my profound appreciation of this honor, coming so unexpectedly as it does. My relations with the other gentlemen who were in nomination were such that I could not without dishonor have entered into the canvass against them. There were other reasons why I could not desire the nomination. I had looked, not without hope and not without ambition, to filling a position in my chosen profession, in which I trusted that I might have served South Carolina, but the call of this Convention, which I recognize as the call of the people of the State, has been made and I appear to answer that call and to discharge the duties you have imposed upon me to the best of my ability.[124]*

Although a candidate for Governor, Hugh Thompson was not the sort of politician who would attract newspaper coverage by playing to the reporters. He never engaged in a display of theatrics. His deportment was straightforward and business-like.

The *New York Times* recognized Hugh Thompson's nomination for Governor on August 11, 1882, writing,

> *Col. Thompson, the nominee for Governor, is unquestionably a Bourbon, but he does not belong to the class of politicians who believe the end justifies the*

---

[123] Thompson, Henry T., *The Establishment of the Public School System*, p. 55.

[124] Thompson, Henry T., *The Establishment of the Public School System*, p. 55.

means. He is more of an educator than a politician, and therefore he is not liked by the bosses and ring politicians, who thrive on the ignorance of their constituents. He administered the affairs of his office as State Superintendent of Education with fairness and ability, and he is considered honorable and high-toned. His nomination is the best and most judicious that could have been made under existing circumstances to prolong Bourbon rule.[125]

"Bourbon Democrat" is a late 19th century term that refers to members of the Democratic party who were ideologically aligned with classical liberalism including fiscal conservatism, free market and laissez-faire economics, limited government and freedom of speech. It especially applied to those supporting President Grover Cleveland, a Democrat.

Hugh Thompson gave a campaign speech at Anderson, South Carolina, on August 31st that laid his priorities for education on the table in no nonsense language that all could understand. Clearly, he would be an education Governor. The *New York Times* quoted him:

We want a school system that is good enough for the rich and cheap enough for the poor. Nothing less than this will satisfy the demands of the times and meet the necessities of the State. An ignorant people cannot long be a free people. In proportion as the structure of a Government gives force to public opinion it is essential that public opinion should be enlightened. If a people expects to be ignorant and free in a state of civilization, it expects what can never be. The learning of the few is despotism. The learning of the many is liberty. An intelligent and principled liberty is fame and wisdom and power. We want the fame, wisdom, and power which will come from the education of the masses. The church and

---

[125] "South Carolina Bourbons, Col. Thompson's Nomination a Victory for the Up-Country Politicians," *The New York Times* (New York), August 11, 1882.

*the school-house must rule this country, and the teachers
in our common schools must be raised to that plane
where they will be useful to society. ... we shall have to
be taxed either for ignorance or education. Every dollar
taken from the schools will go to the support of the jails,
penitentiaries, and poor-houses.*[126]

Hugh Thompson's comprehensive and far-sighted view of
the essential need for education in South Carolina, the United
States, and the world anticipated those of H.G. Wells (1866-
1946) by 40 years. Wells wrote in 1920, "Human history
becomes more a race between education and catastrophe."[127]

His emphatic position regarding the need for educating not
just the white population but also the Black population flew
against the historical pattern going back over 200 years. The
South had not been known for promoting educational excellence
in the white population and had attempted to keep the Black
population from obtaining even rudimentary education.

In the years since the Civil War, the Black population had
little opportunity for an education, and the whites, struggling
through the hard times of Reconstruction, did not rate education
as a priority. Hugh Thompson wanted to make major changes
in the attitudes and availability of educational opportunities for
all. The former slave owner, the Confederate soldier with an
aristocratic background, aggressively promoting education not
just for whites but for Blacks as a requirement for civilization,
was truly visionary.

The election of 1882 featured Hugh S. Thompson running
for Governor against the Greenback Labor party candidate, a
former Red Shirt himself, J. Hendrix McLane. The Greenback
Labor party was an agrarian based party that believed that the
"greenback" money printed without being backed by gold
benefitted farmers.

---

[126] "Education in South Carolina," *The New York Times* (New York),
September 10, 1882.
[127] Wells, H.G., *The Outline of History*, London: Cassell and Company,
1920, reprinted November 1934, p. 1158.

On September 18th Hugh was in Winnsboro, Fairfield County, where he, as usual, made a campaign speech. On the 25th, J. Hendrix McLane appeared at the same location to make a speech of his own. He was attacked by a drunken mob of Democrat supporters and, perhaps, was fortunate to escape with his life.

Shortly after his arrival, McLane, who was accompanied by his little daughter, was greeted by the county Democratic chairman Maj. Thomas W. Woodward after which McLane went to his hotel. It was reported in the Sumter, South Carolina newspaper[128] that

> *as the day wore on the Democrats, clad in red shirts and well mounted, flocked into town from all parts of the country until the courthouse square was thronged with a yelling and enthusiastic crowd.*
>
> *The Democrats grew restive and more excited every hour, and, led on by a few men who had been drinking heavily, the thoroughly incensed throng surged around the hotel and demanded a sight of McLane. Major Woodward went to the courthouse and made a patriotic address, counselling moderation and good order. Returning to the hotel he went to McLane's room, completed the arrangements for the speaking, and locking arms with the desperately nervous Greenbacker, he made a start for the courthouse. As soon as they reached the head of the stairs in the second story McLane was roughly collared by a drunken man and jerked around. Major Woodward promptly rescued him and turned into a narrow passage which led to the hotel parlor. Just as this flank movement was made another man, frenzied with drink, gave McLane a kick. As soon as the party had reached the parlor, the door was shut and a strong guard of Democrats was stationed at the door to prevent any act of violence. As soon as this was*

---

[128] The description of the events is from *The Watchman and Southron* (Sumter, SC), October 3, 1882. *The Watchman* indicates that the article was from "Correspondence of the *News and Courier* [Charleston, SC]."

done and quiet had somewhat been restored, Maj. Woodward with pistol in hand, and quivering all over with anger, went to the hotel balcony and made another ringing address, telling the Democrats that they had placed him at the head of the party in Fairfield , and he demanded of them that they keep the peace and abstain from every act of violence. Many of the most prominent men in the county rallied to Major Woodward's support and determined that they would see that McLane and his party had a fair showing. But the discomforted Greenback refused to leave the parlor.

A squad of men who were wild with drink, and the excitement of the occasion, crowded the passages of the hotel, they massed around the parlor door, but were kept at a safe [safe!] distance by the firmness of the guards. Mounted on chairs and boxes they struggled to look through the transom at the shaking sinner within the parlor, and could not be quieted. At last with a tremendous serge [sic], the parlor door was burst in, and but for the prompt and steady resistance of Maj. Woodward and his aides violent hands would doubtless have been laid on McLane. Finding that all appeals were vain, at last the Sheriff was called and with the aid of a policeman he speedily cleared the hotel of all belligerent persons.

No modern reader would find the newspaper account anything but outrageous and chilling. It must have been terrifying for McLane, "the shaking sinner" as the newspaper called him. The *Intelligencer*, of Anderson, South Carolina wrote

In going to the polls each man should vote according to his honest convictions, and hence should choose between the ticket headed by Hugh S. Thompson and that led by J. Hendrix McLane. In this alternative, but one decision can be reached by any man with self-respect. There is no comparison between the men, and none between their principles. Col. Thompson is a gentleman of ability, integrity and patriotism; McLane is an office seeking, self-asserting demagogue, with no ability and with the most infamous political affiliations. The true men of Carolina will see to it in November that he shall never be Governor of South Carolina by the votes of the people of this State.[129]

This attack on Hendrix McLane is important to the story of Hugh S. Thompson because McLane held Hugh Thompson directly responsible for the attack. This accusation was given nationwide exposure in both the *New York Times* and *Chicago Tribune*.

However, as the newspapers of the day were extremely partisan, there is no reliable, objective period news source where the reader in the 21st century can find unbiased factual news. The southern newspapers, when relating the story of the attack, did not mention McLane's assertion that it was instigated by Hugh Thompson. No eyewitness accounts have been located to either confirm Hugh Thompson's involvement or to exonerate him.

McLane appeared in Washington, DC on October 6th and gave an interview with *The New York Times* and other news outlets. *The Times* quoted McLane:

I arrived at Winnsboro at an early hour...soon after our arrival we were informed that Col. Thompson, Democratic candidate for Governor, had on the 18th while addressing the people at this place publicly said: "You remember the reception you gave Taft here in 1880. Well, when McLane comes here on the 25th give him the same kind of a reception or a worse one." This was received with loud shouts of "We will!" It will be remembered that Taft, a Republican orator, was mobbed at Winnsboro in 1880, his meeting being broken up and he personally assaulted so violently that he would have probably been killed if some of the leading men of the place had not interfered to protect him. Soon after my

---

[129] *The Intelligencer* (Anderson, South Carolina), October 5, 1882.

arrival Col. Woodward, Chairman of the Democratic County Committee of Fairfield County called on me at the hotel.... He admitted that Thompson had used the language attributed to him but that he [Woodward] thought he could control his men if they did not get drunk. He admitted, however, that whisky had been freely given to the red shirters and that they were using it pretty freely, for which he expressed regret.

McLane continued,

Colonel Woodward took my right arm, and my little daughter, who was with me, walked on my left side, having hold of my hand. On reaching the landing on the second floor of the hotel we met a mob of red-shirted Democrats, filling the stairway and corridors. One of these men sprang forward and caught me by the collar of my shirt with such violence as to tear it open. Col. Woodward then threw himself between me and the mob and crowded me back through the hall and into the open door of the hotel parlor, the mob following so closely upon us that one of them kicked me most violently. This was about 12 o'clock noon, and for seven hours it required the utmost efforts and vigilance of several personal Democratic friends to prevent my being mobbed and perhaps murdered. At one time, the parlor door, which was locked, was broken open by the mob and, they were only kept back by my friends holding the door closed from the inside by main strength.[130]

McLane was escorted to the train depot at 7 pm and left town.

The Chicago Tribune published an article very similar to that of *The New York Times* extensively quoting McLane. This article also contains McLane assertion that

---

[130] *The New York Times* (New York), October 7, 1882.

McLane's account for *The Chicago Tribune* also included the comment that Col. Woodward, Chairman of the Democratic County Committee of Fairfield County, "admitted that Thompson had used the language attributed to him, but he [Woodward] thought he could control his men if they did not get drunk."[133]

The 1880 attack on William N. Taft was shrugged off by *The News and Herald* newspaper as an exaggeration of the local Red Shirts hurrahing and shouting. However, the paper did carry the first-person account of the attack written by Taft as it had appeared in the *News and Courier* of Charleston. Taft wrote that he was confronted by hundreds of mounted Red Shirts, shouting and threatening, who charged him in attempts to run him down. They spurred and hit his horse as well as attempting to drag him off his horse. When he spoke he was "interrupted

---

[131] Bourbon Democrat is a late 19th century term that refers to members of the democratic party who were ideologically aligned with fiscal conservatism, and classical liberalism, especially those supporting President Grover Cleveland.

[132] William Nelson Taft (1847-1889) was a carpet-bagger having been born in Rhode Island, serving as a private in the 3rd Rhode Island heavy artillery, 1862-1865. He was stationed at Charleston at the time of his release from the US military. He had various occupations: i.e., bar owner on East Bay, dry goods store owner, Charleston City Alderman, coroner, State Senator 1876-1880, Supervisor for Charleston Schools, Commissioner of the Charleston Orphan Home, and ranks leading to General in the SC Militia, per Bailey N. Louise, *Biographical Directory of the South Carolina Senate, 1776-1985*, vol. III, Columbia: University of SC Press. p. 1575.

[133] *The Chicago Tribune* (Chicago), October 7, 1882.

with profane and obscene epithets, shaking of fists and revolvers at me, declaring that they would kill me before I got away." He asserted that, "but for the personal intervention of Maj. Woodward and Mr. Ellison, at the risk of their own persons, who placed themselves between myself and the mob I would have been instantly killed."[134]

The individual who allegedly told McLane that Hugh Thompson had urged his followers to attack McLane as they had Taft is not identified in either article. Although McLane alleges that Col. Woodward confirmed that Thompson had urged the attack, there is no evidence, other than McLane's statement, that Woodward did so. No evidence has been found indicating that Hugh Thompson responded to McLane's accusation in any way. McLane's accusation may have been his own method of attempting to discredit his political opponent, Hugh Thompson. The actual truth is indeterminable.

Hugh Thompson was elected in 1882 by a large majority, having received 67,158 votes. Hendrix McLane received 17,319 votes.

The salary of the governor was $3500 per year. Hugh and Elizabeth moved into the Governor's Mansion where they had lived after their marriage in 1858 when he was a teacher at the Arsenal Academy. Their first son, Henry Tazewell Thompson, had been born there July 6, 1859. An unpleasant association was that General Sherman had stayed there in February 1865 during the destruction of Columbia.

In 1884, the *News and Courier* newspaper in Charleston reported,

In the campaign of 1882 Governor Thompson made an exceptionally brilliant canvass of the state, from the "blue mountains to the blue sea," gaining everywhere in popular favor, and was elected by a tremendous majority over his weak but wily and unscrupulous competitor, J. Hendrix McLane. His administration during the past two years has been

---

[134] *The News and Herald* (Winnsboro, SC), October 26, 1880, and October 28, 1880.

characterized by excellent judgment. The State has continued to prosper in all her industrial and material resources, the public credit has been maintained, the law has been administered with justice and equity, the public schools have flourished, the races have lived in perfect peace, and a feeling of personal security and public safety has prevailed during an administration which will be notable in the history of the State for the equal satisfaction it has afforded to all the people, without regard to party or section. When the State Democratic Convention met in June last, Governor Thompson was renominated, together with all his associates on the State ticket, without opposition. During the recent canvass he visited every part of the State and electrified the people with his eloquence. He will go into office again, possessing the entire confidence of the people, and better qualified than ever to discharge the important and onerous duties of his high official station.[135]

Hugh Thompson, displaying his sense of humor, told the story of a patient from a lunatic asylum in Columbia who was sometimes allowed the freedom of the town. When Thompson was renominated for Governor, the lunatic met him on the street and, running up to him, grasped him by the hand and said with effusiveness, "I congratulate you, Governor. Everybody in the lunatic asylum is delighted at your renomination."[136]

In November 1883, Hugh Thompson officially gave to the South Carolina Assembly his Annual Message which detailed the status of the State in many areas. The first part of the Message detailed the financial situation including a horrific debt generated in the past. He wrote that the State would require $348,235 to "meet the ordinary expenses of the Government." However, an additional $391,878 "for interest on the public

---

[135] Thompson, Henry T., *The Establishment of the Public School System*. p. 56.
[136] *Daily News* (Frederick, MD), July 27, 1886.

debt" was also needed. Obviously, Hugh Thompson faced not only social challenges as governor, but financial ones as well.

A large portion of the Message concerned the current state of education. 74,157 white and 98,938 "colored" students were enrolled in the public schools, an increase of 27,121 over the preceding year. Based on the 1880 census, this enrollment represented 73 percent of the white children and 55 percent of the Black children between six and sixteen years. It is interesting to find that the average school year was only four months. There were 3,494 teachers of which 2,165 were white and 1,329 were Black, an increase of 81 teachers. The number of schools increased by 86 to 3,269.

The Message stressed the importance of local taxation funding local schools, as "each community knows best its own needs, and its citizens will take more interest in schools established and supported by themselves than in those maintained and controlled by any other authority." Hugh Thompson also pointed out that "the need for good high schools is a pressing one, which becomes each year more apparent."

Claflin College, which still exists as Claflin University, in Orangeburg was organized in 1869 to teach both male and female Black students. Thompson reported that since 1879 thirty students had graduated, 424 students were enrolled the previous year, and the curriculum was expanding.

The Citadel had reopened and in its first year of operation its enrollment was 155 cadets. The academic board consisted of a superintendent, three professors and three assistant professors. The building had been completely repaired. According to the Message, "The aim of the South Carolina Military Academy is now, as it was in the past, to prepare young men for the various callings of life by wholesome discipline, by practical and scientific training, and by the cultivation of all their powers, physical, mental and moral. From the founding of the Academy in 1843 until it was closed in 1865, about 1,800 young men of the State were educated in whole or in part within its walls."

A claim was presented to the Secretary of War for use of, and damage to, the Citadel buildings during the 17 years after the war when it was used by the Federal Government. To date, the State of South Carolina had not received any compensation: "If anything could add strength to this claim, it is the fact that the sum which will be paid by the Federal Government will be used for educational purposes."

The South Carolina College, now the University of South Carolina, had now been repaired and equipped. Its teaching faculty consisted of a president, seven teachers and three tutors. There was an enrollment of 185 students in the past year.

The Institution for the Education of the Deaf and Dumb and the Blind had 72 students enrolled. In addition, a department for the "colored" was established with three students and several more applications had been accepted. His Message stated:

The schools for the white and colored pupils are conducted in different buildings and are separate and distinct, but under the same general management. Pupils are required, according to their means, to pay for their board and tuition in whole or in part; but most of the pupils are unable to contribute to their own support and are maintained at the expense of the State. Special attention is paid in giving the pupils practical instructions in such industrial pursuits as they will be able to follow after leaving the institution. This institution is performing efficiently that important work for which it was designed – the fitting of the afflicted youth of both sexes for the duties of life.

The Lunatic Asylum, as it was called, had 352 white and 254 Black patients. The reports for the past few years indicated an increase of 50 to 60 each year, which was expected to continue.

Hugh S. Thompson's Message provides a look at some of the problems of the prison system and prison reform. The State Penitentiary contained 896 inmates. Very interesting to modern readers is that 55 inmates were white and 841 were Black. The majority of these prisoners were leased out to railroads, farms and other contractors. Abuse was common. Many of the leases were expiring, and the State did not have sufficient prison cells to house all the inmates. The buildings under construction would have about 300 cells designed for one man per cell. Putting two or three men in each cell was not desirable.

Hugh Thompson suggested that the General Assembly, as soon as possible, arrange for trained prison officers to supervise all leased prisoners:

The proper care of large numbers of prisoners requires vigilance, judgment and experience. I am convinced that it is the want of these qualifications on the part of the contractors, rather than deliberate cruelty or willful neglect, that such evils as now exist in the system of leasing convicts in this State are to be ascribed. The great object of prison discipline – the reformation of criminals – cannot be accomplished when convicts are hired to contractors, who fail, either from ignorance or neglect, to perform their duties both in the spirit and the letter of the law. The Penitentiary is not only self-sustaining, but a source of revenue to the State. With proper management it can and will be made so in the future. But the institution is designed to prevent and punish crime, not to swell the public revenue. The increase of revenue sinks into insignificance in comparison with the abuses which I believe will continue to exist while the convicts are hired to work beyond the control of the officers of the penitentiary.

The Governor's Message regarding the militia is of interest considering the militia activities in politics. The "State Volunteer Troops" were white, and the "National Guard" were Black. There were seventy-two companies comprising the State Volunteer Troops with 3,806 men. The National Guard had 4,854 men in nineteen companies. Some companies were cavalry. Hugh Thompson commented that "the present militia force is sufficiently large for all purposes, but its more thorough organization and discipline and increased efficiency are greatly to be desired." Just what role the militia had to play as well as how increased efficiency would benefit the State are left entirely unstated.

Thompson ran unopposed in the 1884 election.

On March 4, 1884, the Thompson's daughter, 18-year-old daughter Eliza Cornelia[137] was badly burned when her dress caught on fire at the Governor's Mansion. She had been sitting by the fire reading. 80 years later, her sister [Caroline Thompson Harrington, (1874-1969)] spoke, with horror, of Eliza being terribly burned. Eliza died on March 15th in the Governor's Mansion at 6 pm from lockjaw. She is buried at Trinity Church in Columbia.

In late May 1886, Hugh S. Thompson received a telegram from Wade Hampton who was serving as U.S. Senator from South Carolina. Hampton suggested that Hugh come to Washington where he was likely to receive an offer of a Federal appointment from Democratic President Grover Cleveland. Hugh met the President at the White House, and they discussed the position of United States Commissioner of Education. He respectfully declined the offer and returned to Columbia.

The newspapers in South Carolina cheered his "unwillingness to resign the office of Governor merely to promote his own interests" and that doing so

> *gives additional evidence of his appreciation of the responsibilities and obligations of the exalted office he now holds. The honor proffered him at Washington, like all the others he has received, came to Governor Thompson without being sought by him, and marks the widespread recognition of his ability and fidelity in the discharge of every trust that has been committed to him. Of the long roll of Governors of the State, none has served South Carolina with more zeal and conscientiousness than the courteous, modest and high-minded gentleman who now fills and graces the Executive office, Gov. Hugh S. Thompson.[138]*

---

[137] Eliza Cornelia Thompson (1866-1884) was born on an unknown date in 1866.

[138] "Keeping Faith with the People," *The Watchman and Southron* (Sumter, SC), June 1, 1886.

Another paper suggested that "we think he would be fully warranted in accepting an important Federal position, being so near the end of his term. It is just such men as Hugh S. Thompson that we want to get into prominent Federal positions."[139]

The view that he should accept the offer was common in the South Carolina press. *The Intelligencer* of Anderson, South Carolina reprinted an editorial published in *The Register* of Columbia:

We feel very well sure that the verdict will be all but universal that no more proper man could be found in the whole country to meet the fullest requirements of the position, and that while all must commend the very refined sense of duty to his State which has compelled him to decline the appointment, there will be a very general feeling of regret that anything should prevent his acceptance of an office where his pre-eminent qualifications for its duties would have enabled him to extend to the educational interest of the country at large the benefits of that ripe experience and enlightened and liberal policy which have under his administration as superintendent of education and governor effected so much for popular education in South Carolina. This country has no purer type of manly patriotism than that which the public and private record of Hugh S. Thompson presents, and it is indeed a hopeful sign when such men are preferred for places of high trust and responsibility to the self-seeking and aspiring horde who crowd the avenues to every public place and are too often foisted into their positions regardless of character

---

[139] *The Abbeville Press and Banner* (Abbeville, SC), June 2, 1886.

*or fitness. It is to be hoped that the barrier to preferment
which Governor Thompson's sense of duty has raised
between him and the broad field of usefulness which
invites him will not exist for long, and constituents may
yet see him placed where he can truly do the most
good.*[140]

The Weekly News and Courier of Charleston opined,
*his administration during the past four years has been
characterized by excellent judgment. The State has
continued to prosper in all her industrial and material
resources, the public credit has been maintained, the
laws have been administered with justice and equity, the
public schools have flourished, the races have lived
together in perfect peace and a feeling of personal
security and public safety has prevailed during an
administration which will be notable in the history of the
state for the equal satisfaction it has afforded to all the
people without regard to party or section.*[141]

It may well be appropriate to remind ourselves of a
sentence from the *Columbia Register*:
*This country has no purer type of manly patriotism
than that which the public and private record of Hugh S.
Thompson presents, and it is indeed a hopeful sign when
such men are preferred for places of high trust and
responsibility to the self-seeking and aspiring horde who
crowd the avenues to every public place and are too
often foisted into their positions regardless of character
or fitness.*

Is it any wonder that the Federal Government, even the
President of the United States, would take notice and come
calling?

---

[140] "The Appointment Tendered to Governor Thompson," *The Intelligencer*
(Anderson, SC), June 3, 1886. Reprint from *Columbia Register*.
[141] *The Weekly News and Courier* (Charleston, SC), July 7, 1886, p. 5.

Chapter 8
1886: Assistant Secretary of the U.S. Treasury

President Cleveland did not forget his meeting with Hugh Thompson. He was again invited to visit the President at the White House a few weeks after his first visit. On this occasion he was offered the post of Assistant Secretary of the Treasury. The position was available as one of the assistant secretaries, William C. Smith, had resigned. The governor had not solicited the position nor had anyone suggested his name to the President, who had acted on his own initiative. The offer was accepted on June 28, 1886.

The Secretary of the Treasury, Daniel Manning, was seriously ill and absent from his post. The responsibilities of the Treasury Department would be handled by Charles S. Fairchild, the senior Assistant Secretary of the Treasury, who would be Acting Secretary of the Treasury with the incoming Hugh Thompson as the Assistant Secretary of the Treasury.

The governor resigned effective July 10, 1886. His term would have ended in December; however, it was likely that he would have been reelected for a third term. Instead, twenty-one years after the defeat of the Confederacy, this former Confederate Captain was in the Yankee capital as an official in the United States government. One wonders what he and Lieze thought of such a twist of fate.

The influential *News and Courier* newspaper of Charleston was enthusiastic about the selection of Hugh Thompson, writing "In the opinion of President Cleveland 'the United States require the services of Governor Thompson, and the Governor feels that he has no right to refuse to enter upon the field of national usefulness which is open to him.'"

The newspaper continued,

The State will lose much in losing Governor Thompson, but the country at large will gain. We congratulate the President upon his selection, which will be fully justified by the event, and we heartily congratulate Governor Thompson on the recognition again accorded him. It is seldom, in a Republic, that they rise rapidly who never seek popularity, but depend for their success, in public life, on their fidelity to public trusts, and upon their ability, their fearlessness and their impartiality in the discharge of their duty. There are exceptions, however, which restore and confirm our faith in our institutions. Governor Thompson was faithful over few things and is made ruler over many things. What was said to Governor Cleveland, when he was notified of his nomination as the Democratic candidate for President, can be said with equal truth to Hugh S. Thompson of South Carolina.[142]

The last sentence refers to Governor Grover Cleveland, upon hearing cannon firing, being told "they are firing a salute in your honor, Governor."

Charles Fairchild asked Hugh Thompson to start his new duties as soon as possible due to the absence of Treasury Secretary Daniel Manning. If his nomination was confirmed by the Senate, he would begin on July 12th.[143]

Hugh Thompson was probably in Washington settling into his new position on August 31, 1886, when Lieze and the rest of the Thompson family were still living in Columbia as one of the most significant earthquakes to occur in South Carolina struck. Their 12-year-old daughter, Caroline, recalled 75 years later the massive devastation. On September 7th, the Governor of New Jersey sent Hugh Thompson, still addressing him as Governor, an offer to send to Charleston 200 wall tents, 35 hospital tents and 500 "A" or wedge tents. Despite no longer being the Governor, Hugh Thompson, no doubt thinking that the

---

[142] *The Weekly News and Courier* (Charleston, SC) July 7, 1886, p. 6-7.
[143] "The State and the Man," *The Weekly News and Courier* (Charleston, SC), July 7, 1886, p. 5-6.

government of South Carolina was busy responding to the disaster, replied asking for the wall tents, hospital tents and 100 "A" tents. To avoid confusion and explanations he signed the telegram as "Governor of South Carolina."[144]

Hugh S. Thompson as Assistant Secretary of the Treasury

There were two Assistant Secretaries of the Treasury. They were of equal rank although one would be considered the First Assistant and the other the Second Assistant. Charles S. Fairchild was the First Assistant but very frequently was the Acting Secretary of the Treasury in the absence of Daniel Manning.

The position of Assistant Secretary of the Treasury ranks just below the cabinet officer level of Secretary of the Treasury. With the illness of Secretary Manning the Assistant Secretaries' positions were considered to be elevated in status.

The work of the Treasury department was divided among various divisions or bureaus, all of which were under the

---

[144] "Tents for Charleston," *Courier-Post* (Camden, New Jersey), September 8, 1886, p. 1.

direction and control of the Assistant Secretaries. Hugh Thompson would have "control of all appointments under the Treasury Department and will have charge besides of the Divisions of Public Moneys; of Warrants, Estimates and Appropriations; Stationery, Printing and Blanks; Loans and Currency; Mail and Files; the Bureau of Printing and Engraving, and the office of the Director of the Mint. In addition, the Assistant Secretary signs all letters and papers relating to the business of his divisions and bureaus which do not, by law, require the signature of the Secretary himself."[145]

The wide range of Hugh Thompson's duties ran from the seemingly trivial to those involving vast sums of money. One citizen mailed him a silver half dollar that had been worn smooth and wondered if it was still legal tender. Hugh Thompson sent the coin back and advised that per the department regulations of August 1, 1887, mutilated coins were no longer acceptable but that "reduction by natural abrasion is not considered mutilation."[146]

Hugh Thompson's office in the Treasury Building was on the southeast corner on the second floor – not including the basement or ground floor. The back of $10 bills made between 1928 and 2000 feature the southeast corner of the Treasury Building with his office windows clearly visible. The bills made

---

[145] "Governor Thompson to be the Assistant Secretary of the Treasury," *The Weekly News and Courier* (Charleston, SC), July 7, 1886, p. 6.
[146] *Fort Scott Daily Tribune* (Fort Scott, KS), May 9, 1888, p. 6.

since 2000 bear the image of the Treasury Building as seen face-on from the south. On those his office windows are obscured by a tree. My father identified Hugh Thompson's office location for me. Undoubtedly, he was given the information from his mother, Caroline Thompson Harrington who would have been fifteen when her father was Assistant Secretary of the Treasury.

Despite having been in Washington for a year, Hugh Thompson was invited to attend the unveiling of a statue of John C. Calhoun in Charleston in April 1887. He sent his regrets saying that "important public duties" would prevent him from being present. However, he softened the message by saying that, "if it were possible for me to attend it would give me sincere pleasure to witness the ceremonies which will make the consummation of the great work which will stand for all time to commemorate the virtues of the patriot and statesman, as well as the zeal and devotion of the noble women to whom South Carolina is indebted for this memorial of her most illustrious son."[147]

The Secretary of the Treasury placed advertisements in newspapers seeking contractor bids for such things as cleaning the carpets, towels, lumber, ice, and file holders for the Treasury Department. Notices seeking bids for furniture for Post Offices, as well as minor and major office building renovations, were common. Other notifications pertained to buildings and properties. He would also respond to queries from individuals and organizations interested in obtaining funds for projects authorized by various Acts of Congress. One notice sought bids for 25 jurors' chairs, which were to be placed in various government buildings.[148]

---

[147] Letter of Hugh S. Thompson to Mrs. George Robertson, April 23, 1887, in *A History of the Calhoun Monument at Charleston, SC*, 1888 published by the Ladies Calhoun Monument Association, p. 129. The monument was unveiled April 26, 1887. It was replaced in 1896 with a statue in Marion square, which was taken down in 2020.

[148] *National Republican* (Washington, DC), May 25, 1887, p. 3. *San Francisco Chronicle* (San Francisco, CA), May 29, 1887, p. 16. *Boston Post* (Boston, MA), May 30, 1887, p. 5. *Washington Sentinel* (Washington, DC), September 3, 1887, p. 2. *The Boston Globe* (Boston, MA), September 19, 1887, p. 7.

In August 1887, Hugh Thompson accompanied the Superintendent of the Life Saving Service of the United States on a three-week tour of inspection of life-saving stations, lighthouses, and revenue cutters on the Great Lakes. Hugh Thompson was apparently observing the efficiency of the Customs Service. He is quoted by the *Detroit Free Press* saying, "We have left the mouth of the Niagara River bound for Duluth and are pressing on as fast as possible. All our leisure, if we have any, will be on the way home. Then we hope to see very much more of the beautiful cities on the lake than is now possible. Do you know this is my first knowledge of the lake country and it is a revelation to me. I am very anxious to see more of it, and I sincerely hope that we may have time to do it."[149]

Incongruously, in May 1887, articles appeared in South Carolina newspapers expressing the desire that, if the current president of South Carolina College resigned, Hugh Thompson would return to Columbia and take up the position. It was suggested that he "would arouse a new enthusiasm for the College." One wonders why it was thought he would return.[150]

Very curiously the position of Commissioner of Fisheries was apparently offered to Hugh Thompson by President Cleveland in September 1887. The newspaper wryly pointed out that if Thompson "possesses any exhaustive knowledge of ichthyology or any other branch of natural science he had succeeded admirably in concealing this fact from his fellow citizens."[151] How astonishing it would have been had he accepted the position.

The 1880's brought a recession to the U.S.[152] In a successful move to strengthen public confidence in the

---

[149] "A Revelation to Him", *Detroit Free Press* (Detroit, MI), August 3, 1887, p. 8. "The Life Saving Service," *The New York Times* (New York), August 23, 1887, p. 1.

[150] *The Intelligencer* (Anderson, SC), May 12, 1887.

[151] *St. Louis Globe-Democrat* (St. Louis, MO), September 3, 1887, p. 4.

[152] Michael D. Bordo & Joseph G. Haubrich, *Deep Recessions, Fast Recoveries, and Financial Crises: Evidence from the American Record*, 2013, available from

Government and avoid a financial crisis, James W. Hyatt, the Treasurer, and Hugh S. Thompson, in the role of Acting Secretary of the Treasury in the absence of Charles Fairchild, met with President Cleveland at the White House until 11 pm on the night of September 21, 1887. It was decided that the Government would buy $14 million in U.S. bonds. The notice was issued around midnight averting the crisis.[153]

The Thompsons lived at 1514 K Street NW when they first came to Washington in the summer of 1886.[154] On October 2, 1887, the family moved into a leased residence at 1206 P-Street Northwest in Washington, DC with 13-year-old Caroline, 14-year-old Elizabeth and 15-year-old Hugh S. Thompson, Jr. They lived next door to Teddy Roosevelt. This was 10 years prior to Roosevelt's exploits at San Juan Hill in the Spanish-American War. On the other side was Union Brigadier General William S. Rosecrans (1819-1898), who had been badly defeated at the Battle of Chickamauga in 1863. Beyond Rosecrans lived Adlai E. Stevenson (1835-1914), the First Assistant United States Postmaster General. In 1893-1897 Stevenson was Vice President under President Grover Cleveland.[155]

Throughout their time in Washington the Thompsons were frequently in the newspapers, which noted their attendance at various social gatherings or activities, such as "Mrs. Thompson will be at home on Wednesday during the season beginning in December." The newspapers would also mention social items such as "Miss Thompson is still in Charleston, SC and will not be back in the city before December." They were referring to

---

https://jrc.princeton.edu/sites/g/files/toruqf2471/files/jrcppf_2013_-_bordo_-_paper.pdf .

[153] "Government Bonds," *Chattanooga Daily Times* (Chattanooga, TN), September 22, 1887, p. 1. "Calling in the Bonds, Preventing a Much Feared Money Famine," *The Grand Island Daily Independent* (Grand Island, NB), September 22, 1887, p. 1.

[154] *Washington, DC City Directory*, 1887.

[155] *Evening Star* (Washington, DC), October 4, 1887, p. 1. Thompson, Thomas Clarkson, *The Narratives of Thomas Clarkson Thompson, 1860-1938*, edited and annotated by H. T. Harrington, 31-32.

Elizabeth Clarkson "Elise" Thompson (1872-1942), Hugh's daughter. When "Secretary and Mrs. Fairchild gave their third card reception" they "received their guests in the library" where "Mrs. Fairchild wore a demi-trained dress of wild-rose brocade trimmed with cuffs and revers of olive brocade." Among the numerous guests at this Gilded Age event was "Mrs. Hugh S. Thompson, black lace and net."[156]

In a similar vein, but perhaps oddly intrusive and obscure, when Hugh Thompson's son John visited his uncle Edgar L. Clarkson in Birmingham Alabama, the local *Birmingham Age* newspaper announced the visit remarking that Hugh S. Thompson was ex-governor of South Carolina and currently Assistant Secretary of the Treasury.[157]

In 1888, the Thompsons were visited by their son Henry Thompson, "editor and proprietor of the Darlington News. Editor Thompson had a pleasant call upon President Cleveland."[158] Such is fame.

In October 1888, Hugh Thompson was subjected to a blistering partisan attack in a few newspapers. He had issued a financial statement showing the amount of surplus the Government had collected over the expenditures for the year. It was a Presidential election year and some newspapers believed that the figures used were inflated to make the current administration appear in a more positive position.

The Indianapolis Journal, under the headline "Thompson's Surplus, A Democratic Paper Dissects His Figures, and Says He Is Unworthy of His Office," wrote that Hugh S. Thompson "with the fatuous zeal of a superserviceable subordinate" presented "an enormous surplus for the present year." Perhaps to arouse sectional bias the article three times pointed out that Thompson was from South Carolina. Phrases such as "figure-juggling performance, with its obvious intention to deceive hardly requires serious treatment" and "in point of dishonesty it is on a level with any prospectus or annual

---

[156] *Evening Star* (Washington, DC), February 8, 1888, p. 1.
[157] *The Birmingham Age* (Birmingham, AL), August 1, 1887, p. 4.
[158] *The Morning News* (Savannah, GA), November 19, 1888.

statement ever issued by any fraudulent railroad corporation or wildcat mining company."

The article stated "...it rivals the efforts of those free-trade editors and orators... for Mr. Thompson deliberately invents for campaign purposes a new a perverted method of computing surplus..." and "...deliberately misrepresents known facts." It continued with "the Southern free-trade sympathizer Assistant Secretary Thompson proceeds in his superserviceable zeal to construct on paper an artificial surplus to mislead our legislators..." In conclusion, "this Mr. Thompson, of South Carolina, is not worthy to hold an office of public trust."[159]

Three weeks later James G. Blaine, in a speech, said, "I find that there has been $60,000,000 loaned to the national banks without interest. I say loaned to the national banks, the pet banks, while only $4,500,000 have gone to pay the debt of the nation during the past month." James G. Blaine (1830-1893), a founder of the Republican Party, had been Secretary of State under President James A. Garfield in 1881 and continued under Chester A. Arthur after Garfield was assassinated. He was the Republican candidate for President in 1884 and lost to Grover Cleveland. In 1888 he supported the candidacy of Benjamin Harrison. After Harrison's victory he was again appointed Secretary of State in 1889.

A reporter from the *New York Herald* went to the then Acting Secretary of the Treasury Hugh Thompson's residence to get his reaction to the statement made by Blaine. He reported that Hugh Thompson read the paragraph carefully, and then with great deliberation said,

This is of a piece with the many other willful misrepresentations which Mr. Blaine has made about the treasury department. No man who has been as long in public life as Mr. Blaine, and who is as familiar with public matters as he, could have made that statement and believed it to be true when he made it. Mr. Blaine's

---

[159] "Thompson's Surplus," *The Indianapolis Journal* (Indianapolis, IN), October 20, 1888, p. 7. Imposing on the Public, Chicago Tribune (Chicago, IL), October 24, 1888, p. 9.

Hugh Thompson continued regarding a charge that
$60,000,000 of the fund had been provided to re-elect President
Cleveland by saying, "That is too absurdly false to dignify with
a denial."[160] In sum, Hugh Thompson pulled no punches and
publicly called Mr. Blaine a liar without using the word.

President Cleveland was defeated in his bid for reelection
on November 6, 1888, by Benjamin Harrison. This created a
serious difficulty for Hugh Thompson as his position was an
appointment and the new administration would want to reward
their own party faithful with the job. The first indication that he
might be appointed to the Civil Service Commission appeared
on December 6th. The Civil Service Commission was required
to have a Democrat member, and it was thought that he might
land that position.[161]

Meanwhile, the society column of the newspaper noted
that Elizabeth, Hugh Thompson's wife, would be "at home on
Fridays at her residence, 1206 P-Street and will receive with
Mrs. Fairchild on New Year's Day and on Wednesdays during
the season." [162] Apparently the ladies were close. The
importance of the social activities of the gentlemen, as well as
their ladies, should not be underestimated. Mrs. Fairchild, of
course, was the wife of Charles S. Fairchild, the Secretary of the
Treasury. He and Hugh Thompson had been working together

---

[160] "Blaine Given the Lie, Hugh S. Thompson Shows the Utter Falsity of
the Statements of the Plumed Knave Respecting the Treasury," *The
Manning Times* (Manning, SC), November 14, 1888, p. 2 quoting the *New
York Herald*. Also, *Helena Semi-Weekly Herald* (Helena, MT), October 18,
1888, p. 3.
[161] "A Good Man's Good Fortune," *The Intelligencer* (Anderson, SC),
December 13, 1888.
[162] *Evening Star* (Washington, DC) December 29, 1888, December 31,
1888.

for the last couple of years. Fairchild would resign at the end of Cleveland's term in 1889.

Hugh Thompson and a group of friends of Fairchild presented an oil portrait of Fairchild to the Treasury Department in the Spring of 1890.[163] Charles Fairchild was no longer in the government. He would be elected Chairman of the Board of Trustees of the New York Life Insurance Company. This move by Fairchild is important as later he would hire Hugh Thompson to work for New York Life.

President Grover Cleveland wanted Hugh Thompson to land a position on the Civil Service Commission. To make room for him he tried to get Alfred P. Edgerton to resign. When Edgerton refused to resign, Cleveland exercised his option and removed him with a one sentence note, "Dear Sir - You are hereby removed from the office of the United States Civil Service Commission." Cleveland then nominated Hugh Thompson. The removal of Edgerton did not go down well with everyone.

The New York Tribune wrote that

It looks as if the whole plan of providing for Thompson would miscarry altogether, for the Senate is in no temper either to help the President in carrying out his little scheme of paying private political obligations at the public expense or to confirm for such a place as that of Civil Service Commissioner a South Carolina Democrat, and one of Mr. Thompson's antecedents [background] *and record as a spoilsman* [a person who aids a political party in order to share in the spoils] *in the Treasury Department, especially.*

… There is every good reason for believing that the Senate will refuse to confirm Mr. Thompson. Mr. Thompson's record in the Treasury Department where he was in charge of all the appointments has been that of a consistent spoilsman. He never in his life was suspected of being either in sympathy with Civil Service

---

[163] "A Portrait of Ex-Secretary Fairchild," *Evening Star* (Washington, DC) May 13, 1890, p. 1.

principles, or to look with anything but disfavor upon a law which kept Southern patriots from feeding at the public crib. While Edgerton was probably everything that his own characterization of himself implied – to wit, a Democrat – he, at least, never pretended to be anything else. This, certainly, is more than can be said of Hugh S. Thompson.[164]

To be in politics, or to survive in politics, takes a thick skin and a strong man.

The *St. Louis Post-Dispatch*, with the headline "He Walked the Plank, Judge Edgerton Removed from the Civil Service Commission," also covered the story but slightly differently, writing,

The resignation or removal of Edgerton has been expected for some time past. Mr. Edgerton has never been in accord with his colleagues of the commission. ... His indifference not to say hostility, to the work over which he as President of the Civil Service Commission was his duty to preside, has been shown by his habitual absences from office and duty, some of his periods of absence extending over six months.

The *St. Louis Post-Dispatch* reported that Edgerton "said today that his [Edgerton's] removal was mainly to make room for an incompetent man [Hugh Thompson] who had done more than any other to load his department [Treasury Department] down with unreconstructed rebels." But the *Post-Dispatch* continued, "it is quite likely that the Senate will confirm the nomination of Mr. Thompson. Mr. Thompson has become quite popular as a public official in Washington. He was on record as an earnest and intelligent advocate of civil service reform before he came here." The article concludes, "Gov. Thompson does not want to go back to South Carolina and Mrs. Thompson

---

[164] "Mr. Edgerton Removed, Paying a Private Score at the Public Expense," *New York Tribune* (New York), February 10, 1889, p. 11.

especially says she would not leave Washington for anything."[165]

President Cleveland nominated Hugh Thompson for the position of the Democratic member of the United States Civil Service Commission. However, the Republicans, who held the majority in the U.S. Senate, were not accepting any of President Cleveland's nominations, which allowed the incoming Republican President, Benjamin Harrison, to make his own choices. Regardless, Harrison's choice also turned out to be Hugh Thompson.

---

[165] "He Walked the Plank," *St. Louis Post-Dispatch* (St. Louis, MO), February 10, 1889, p. 4.

Chapter 9
1889: U.S. Civil Service Commission

In political circles and among the public, it was considered appropriate that public offices should be used as rewards for political service. The Civil Service Commission dealt with Civil Service Reform, which had real consequences. It made efforts to restore to government three vital values. Firstly, job opportunities would be available to all citizens, not just those of the party in power. Second, only those with qualifications and merit be appointed to government positions. Third, public servants should not be penalized or intimidated for their political beliefs.

President Harrison, on May 7, 1889, sent the nomination of Hugh S. Thompson, now fifty-three years old, as the Democratic member of the Civil Service Commission to the Senate. The nomination was confirmed. Thirty-year-old Theodore Roosevelt, a Republican, was confirmed at the same time. Roosevelt and Hugh Thompson had been next-door neighbors on P-Street in 1887. They joined Republican Charles Lyman who had been appointed in 1886 and was president of the Commission. The influence of Charles Lyman would soon be challenged by a zealous and crusading Theodore Roosevelt. In September Roosevelt wrote Henry Cabot Lodge, "Thank Heaven I have Thompson for a colleague. Lyman is a good, honest, hardworking, man, very familiar with the law; but he is also the most intolerably slow of all the men who have loved red tape."[166]

Both Teddy Roosevelt and Hugh Thompson were strong advocates of civil service reform promoting merit rather than

---

[166] Lodge, Henry Cabot, *Selections from the Correspondence of Theodore Roosevelt and Henry Cabot Lodge, 1884-1918*, New York: Charles Scribner's Sons, 1925. vol. 1, p. 92.

political favoritism to decide the selection of officeholders. However, the Civil Service Commission, and the three Commissioners, were not popular with many politicians nor with those who had been given jobs that they were either incapable of performing or simply failed to perform through lack of will or incentive. Some major newspapers such as the *Washington Post* were against Civil Service reform.

Roosevelt wrote to his good friend Henry Cabot Lodge and his wife, "Dear Nannie and Cabot," on June 12th after having been confirmed as a Civil Service Commissioner. He apparently had not found accommodations as he was staying in the Lodge home, 1211 Connecticut Avenue. The Lodges were away from the city and Roosevelt mentioned to them that "tonight I dine at the Thompson's."[167] From the context it is deduced that his wife, Edith, was not in Washington and therefore would not attend dinner with Hugh and Elizabeth Thompson. It may be assumed that the Thompsons' daughters, Caroline, age 15, and Elizabeth, age 16, and perhaps son Hugh, age 17, were present. In his book, *Selections from the Correspondence of Theodore Roosevelt and Henry Cabot Lodge, 1884-1918*, Henry Cabot Lodge identified Hugh Thompson with the footnote, "Ex-Governor Hugh Thompson of South Carolina, a member of the Civil Service Commission, a most admirable man. He became a close friend of Roosevelt."[168] It is pleasing to find the friendship between Roosevelt and Hugh Thompson confirmed by Henry Cabot Lodge, Roosevelt's best friend.

The three Civil Service Commissioners embarked, on June 17, 1889, on a investigatory tour of some of the post offices in the Great Lakes area. They were looking for corruption, incompetence and partisanship among the postmasters. Their first stop was in Indianapolis where the local postmaster was a

---

[167] Lodge, Henry Cabot, *Selections from the Correspondence of Theodore Roosevelt and Henry Cabot Lodge, 1884-1918*, New York: Charles Scribner's Sons, 1925. vol. 1, p. 77-78. In footnote Lodge clarifies that "he was living in my house."

[168] Lodge, Henry Cabot, *Selections from the Correspondence of Theodore Roosevelt and Henry Cabot Lodge, 1884-1918*, New York: Charles Scribner's Sons, 1925. vol. 1, p. 78.

friend of Republican President Benjamin Harrison. The postmaster had allegedly hired three incompetent men simply because they were Republicans. Thompson, Lyman and Roosevelt investigated and demanded that the men be fired. The postmaster objected but could not overrule the commissioners. President Harrison may have been shocked that his two Republican commissioners joined with Thompson, their Democrat colleague, in removing the three men.

At the next stop, Milwaukee, the three commissioners investigated and then wrote a strongly worded report saying the postmaster himself "has grossly and habitually violated the law, and has done it in a peculiarly revolting and underhanded manner."[169] The commissioners became thorns in the side of many politicians and struck fear into those who had violated the law.

In the fall of 1889, the Thompsons moved "for the season" from the 1206 P-Street Northwest house to an apartment at 1332 Massachusetts Avenue. The newspapers' society news announced that Mrs. Thompson would be at home on Wednesdays during the season beginning in December. Miss Thompson (referring to Elizabeth "Elize," age 16) was still in Charleston, SC and would not be back in the city before December.[170] Fifteen-year-old Caroline would be living at home with her parents.

About the same time Theodore Roosevelt moved into a house at 1820 Jefferson Place, a 20-minute walk from the Thompsons'; his wife Edith and their new-born son Kermit remained at their "country place," Sagamore Hill in Oyster Bay, New York.[171] As the Thompsons and Roosevelts were friends, it is probable they visited each other's homes. The Thompsons apparently moved again, since in January 1891 it was reported that Mrs. Thompson of "Connecticut Avenue and DeSales

---

[169] Morris, Edmund, *The Rise of Theodore Roosevelt*, New York: Coward, McCann & Geoghegan, Inc, 1979, p. 402-407.

[170] *Evening Star* (Washington, DC), October 2, 1889, November 6, 1889, p. 2.

[171] *Evening Star* (Washington, DC), November 6, 1889, p. 2.

Street" would be a hostess at an event.[172] Unless the Roosevelts had also moved, this location was a 6-minute walk to the home of Teddy and Edith Roosevelt in Jefferson Place.

January was an exciting month for the Thompson family. An invitation[173] was received:

The President and Mrs. Harrison
request the pleasure of the company of
Mr. Thompson
and the ladies of his family
on Tuesday evenings January 14th & 28th and February 11th
from nine to eleven o'clock.
1890.

January 14th. To meet the Diplomatic Corps.
" 28th. Reception to the Congress and the Judiciary.
February 11th. To meet the Officers of the Army and Navy and Marine Corps.

Doubtless Elizabeth "Elise" age 17, and Caroline age 15, would attend with their parents. We would certainly like to know what private conversation passed between former Confederates, Hugh and Elizabeth, after such an event.

In January 1890 it was reported in a few South Carolina newspapers that Hugh Thompson would soon be made superintendent of The Citadel.[174] This item sounds more like wishful thinking than a possibility. In June it was rumored that he was being considered, but "not encouraged by him," for appointment as a customs appraiser.[175] In June of 1891, a similar item appeared suggesting that he may become the

---

[172] *Evening Star* (Washington, DC), January 1891, p. 3.
[173] Invitation. In the collection of Joan Harrington Clayton.
[174] *The Intelligencer* (Anderson, SC), June 12, 1890, p. 2.
[175] *The Newberry Herald and News* (Newberry, SC), Jun 19, 1890, p. 1.

president of the college of North Carolina, now the University of North Carolina.[176]

Caroline B. Thompson, daughter of Hugh S. Thompson, at about the time of President Harrison's reception

Meanwhile, former Confederate General, the current South Carolina Senator, Matthew Butler introduced a bill in January 1890 that would be considered outrageously racist in the

---

[176] *Hartford Courant* (Hartford, CT), June 4, 1891, p. 4.

21st century as well as by most people in the 19th century. The bill would compel some Black citizens in the South to emigrate to Africa in exchange for Federal aid. This was a scheme of "assisted emigration" that would reduce the numbers of Blacks in the Black-majority southern states. Efforts would be made to keep the "more industrious, sober, peaceable, and provident" and rid the country of "those to whom none of these adjectives applies."

According to *The New York Times*, this plan "is the best solution that many of the most thoughtful and patriotic among [the Southern whites] can suggest. Whoever opposes it is bound, it seems either to propose another solution of his own or to show that the question is not really so formidable as it is considered to be by those who are in the best position to judge."

As Hugh Thompson was a prominent Southerner in Washington, *The Times* approached him for his opinion. He expressed "himself as strongly opposed to the plan." When asked if he had anything to propose he replied, "the exercise of kindness and forbearance." *The Times* suggested that "this will hardly be satisfactory to the supporters of Senator Butler's bill."[177] The bill did not pass.

Hugh Thompson was a powerful speaker. His public speaking had doubtless come a long way from the Citadel commencement address of 1856 when he "gave full scope for the exercise of the young speaker's oratorical powers, and he improved the occasion to much advantage, and fully came up to the expectations of the audience."[178] He gave a very impressive speech before the House investigating committee in May 1890 that drew some very positive attention to himself.

The *Commercial Advertiser* newspaper of Boston wrote that

> *The Civil Service Commission...have found an orator whose powers heretofore remained unknown to the public, except perhaps in his own State.*

---

[177] "The Negro Question," *The New York Times* (New York), January 21, 1890.

[178] *Charleston Mercury*, November 22, 1856, p. 3.

Commissioner Thompson's argument before the committee created a sensation by its remarkable eloquence and power. It was not merely a fine speech and an able argument, it was a remarkable example of oratory in the best meaning of the word. It astonished the committee and has caused considerable talk. The same speech made in a large assemblage, not confined to the narrow limits of a committee room, would insure his reputation as one of the finest of Southern orators, if not the very finest. Senator Lodge, of Massachusetts, who is generally inclined to be cynical, became enthusiastic while listening to the speech, and said it was an unanswerable argument, and one of the best examples of simple eloquence he had ever heard.[179]

The October 1890 issue of *The Century Illustrated Monthly Magazine* carried an article by Hugh Thompson, titled "The Merit System." This is the only article he is known to have written and published in the popular press. The article discusses the benefits of the merit system in determining qualifications for civil service employment.[180]

Elizabeth Clarkson Thompson was a lifelong advocate for the Confederacy. She did what she could to support the war effort at home and the soldiers at the front during the war. Later she decorated their graves. In 1891, she learned that there were "a considerable number" of former Confederate soldiers in the Washington area that were in great need of assistance. She, along with like-minded southern women, organized an organization called The Woman's Auxiliary Ex-Confederate Aid Society. She was the President. The Society would stage a variety of events including concerts, literary entertainment, a fair, and a supper with dancing "for young people," all of which

---

[179] Thompson, Henry T., *The Establishment of the Public School System of South Carolina.* Columbia, SC: The R.L. Bryan Company, 1927, p. 59. *The Times and Democrat* (Orangeburg, SC) May 28, 1890, p. 4.

[180] Thompson, Hugh S., "The Merit System," *The Century Illustrated Monthly Magazine*, vol. 40, issue 6, New Series vol. XVIII, May 1890-Oct. 1890, New York: The Century Company, 1890, p. 954-956.

were to raise money. The ladies anticipated "substantial assistance" from the surrounding area including Maryland and Virginia.[181]

Hugh Thompson gave a toast at the Sons of the American Revolution banquet on January 16, 1892, celebrating the 1781 victory at Cowpens. A couple of months earlier he had spoken at a Masonic banquet on the subject, "Our Government."[182] Regrettably, these along with so many other short, and long, speeches were never written down and are now lost.

---

[181] "To Help Needy Confederates," *The Baltimore Sun* (Baltimore, MD), November 10, 1891, p. 3. *The Courier-Journal* (Louisville, KY), November 11, 1891, p. 1. *The Washington Post* (Washington, DC), November 13, 1891, p. 6.
[182] *The Wilmington Morning Star* (Wilmington, NC), January 17, 1892, p. 4. *The Sunday Herald* (Washington, DC), November 8, 1891, p. 10.

Chapter 10
1892: Comptroller of New York Life Insurance Company

During the Spring of 1892, New York Life Insurance Company reorganized. The former Secretary of the U.S. Treasury, Charles S. Fairchild, was made chairman of the Board of Trustees. The position of Comptroller was created and offered to Hugh Thompson. He called on President Benjamin Harrison on April 17, 1892, and formally resigned his position as Civil Service Commissioner to take effect on May 15th. He would retain his new position with New York Life until his death.[183]

The New York Times carried an unsigned article, or editorial, concerning the resignation of Hugh S. Thompson:

Mr. Thompson's Resignation
Loss to the Public Service of a True and Devoted Servant

Washington, April 17 – The public service never had a truer or more devoted servant than it will lose in the withdrawal of the Hon. Hugh S. Thompson from the United States Civil Service Commission. Washington has never had a more genial or public-spirited citizen. The New York Life and New York City will gain a good man and a valuable citizen, as the United States loses a capable and conscientious executive officer.

Many persons in this city regret that Mr. Thompson has severed his connection with the branch of the service with which he has always been in sincere sympathy, but all who know Mr. Thompson are glad of his good fortune in entering a calling in which the rewards are sure to be greater and certainly more adequate to his deserts than anything he might be expected to

---

[183] *The National Tribune* (Washington, DC), April 7, 1892, p. 7. *The Baltimore Sun* (Baltimore, MD), April 18, 1892, p. 1.

secure in the way of official appointment even from an Administration with which he was in full political sympathy. It will not take long for his new acquaintances in the metropolis to find out, what his old friends have long known, that, though a South Carolinian by the accident or good fortune of birth, Gov. Thompson is an American, and that there is no State in the Union in which he will not be at home [emphasis added]. *His services in the Civil Service Commission, as his associates will acknowledge, have been more valuable than it would be easy to tell without appearing to be invidious and extravagant in praise. It is safe to say that President Harrison not only made no mistake when he selected him as the Democratic member, but that he could scarcely have found a more fitting representative. To fill his place is a most difficult task.*

Civil Service Commissioner Roosevelt paid a high tribute to Mr. Thompson this afternoon. "Personally," he said, "and for the sake of the public service, I keenly regret that Gov. Thompson is to leave the commission, but I heartily congratulate the New York Life on having secured his services. I have now been associated with him for three years on the commission and our relations have been most intimate. I can say that I have never, in political, business, or social life, met an abler or more high-minded man [emphasis added]. *It would be difficult to place too high a value upon the service Mr. Thompson has rendered to the Civil Service Commission. Before joining the commission, he had shown his very unusual capacity in dealing with financial and business matters while Assistant Secretary of the Treasury, and his record as State Superintendent of Education, and later as Governor of South Carolina, gave him an extended reputation in the South. He is an absolutely fearless and manly man, conscientious to a degree, with great tact in dealing with men; a hard worker and possessed of a ready grasp of all financial and business subjects* [emphasis added]. *The public service suffers a great loss when he leaves it, but it would be hard to imagine a better officer for the exact position to which he has been appointed by the New York Life.* "[184]

Such praise from one of the country's leading newspapers is praise indeed. "No state in the union in which he will not be at home" declares openly that Hugh Thompson, while he would always be a southerner, had risen above regionalism in a country still divided north and south. He had become a true universal citizen. His tact, work ethic and fearless conduct truly makes him a man's man standing out above the crowd.

As comptroller, Hugh Thompson became the high-level officer responsible for the financial and accounting reporting of New York Life Insurance Company. He would remain as comptroller until his death in 1904.

---

[184] "Mr. Thompson's Resignation, Loss to the Public Service of a True and Devoted Servant," *The New York Times* (New York), April 18, 1892. Underlining added for emphasis.

Chapter 11
Teddy Roosevelt and Hugh Thompson

Roosevelt's and Hugh Thompson's relationship continued after Hugh's resignation from the Civil Service Commission in 1892, as shown by Roosevelt's promoting of Thompson's membership in The Century Association.[185] The Century Association was, and is, an exclusive private social club, a gathering place for artists and writers, in New York City. It is "composed of authors and amateurs of Letters and the Fine Arts, residents of the City of New York and its vicinity: its objects the cultivation of a taste for Letters and the Arts and social enjoyment."

The membership has included noted writers and poets as well as a handful of U.S. Presidents, Supreme Court Justices and Nobel Prize Laureates. Mark Twain called the Century Association "the most unspeakably respectable club in New York." He was not a member. Until the late 20th century, it was only for gentlemen. The Century was founded in 1847 and is still in existence located at 7 West 43rd Street in New York.

On February 1, 1896, Hugh Thompson was elected to the Century. He had been proposed for membership by Theodore Roosevelt who was serving at the time as President of the New York City Board of Police Commissioners. The nomination was seconded by the journalist Edward Cary. Cary was a long-time editor of the *New York Times* where he campaigned against the corrupt Tweed Ring. He also was instrumental in fighting for Civil Service Reform. It seems likely that Teddy Roosevelt asked Edward Cary to second Hugh Thompson's nomination as

---

[185] Theodore Roosevelt resigned from the Civil Service Commission in May 1895 to become Police Commissioner of New York City.

he knew Cary would be familiar with Hugh Thompson through his work on the Civil Service Commission.

Edward Cary, wrote after Hugh Thompson's death in 1904, a short memorial for The Century. The first line states, "Hugh Smith Thompson was of the finest type of the Southern Gentleman." After a summary of Hugh's career Cary wrote, "Absorbing business cares and delicate health prevented Mr. Thompson from frequent attendance at The Century, but he leaves here a large circle of warm friends with whom affectionate appreciation of his winning personal qualities is joined to hearty respect for his sterling and enlightened service in his varied public career."[186]

It is tempting to conclude that Teddy Roosevelt, dispensing political favors, nominated many of his friends, or political allies, for membership in The Century. However, it is indicative of the friendship between TR and Hugh Thompson that in his 35 years of membership Roosevelt nominated only seven men.

Roosevelt wrote Henry Cabot Lodge in 1895, "I make acquaintances very easily, but there are only one or two people in the world, outside my own family, whom I deem friends or for whom I really care."[187] Hugh S. Thompson was one of those friends. The close friendship between Teddy Roosevelt and Hugh Thompson continued through the years after Hugh Thompson left the Civil Service Commission in 1892, as shown by Roosevelt's Century club nomination of Hugh Thompson in 1896.

Further evidence of the close friendship, and respect, between Hugh and TR is a letter Roosevelt sent to Hugh dated April 20, 1897. Roosevelt had resigned his position as President of the New York City Board of Police Commissioners on April 19th and had begun his work as Assistant Secretary of the Navy in Washington, having been appointed by President McKinley.

---

[186] Centuryarchives.org

[187] "Letter Theodore Roosevelt to Henry Cabot Lodge, October 11, 1895," *Selections From the Correspondence of Theodore Roosevelt and Henry Cabot Lodge*, New York: Charles Scribner's Sons, 1925, vol. 1, p. 183.

The complete letter:

April 20, 1897
Hon. Hugh S. Thompson
70 East Fifty-fourth Street
New York City, NY

My Dear Governor:
I was awfully sorry to miss you. There is no one I was more anxious to see and say good bye to than you. Lodge, Jacob Riis and Proctor are the three men who, in my judgment, share your pedestal. I am sure you sympathized with my coming here. I have about done all I could in New York.

Faithfully yours,
Theodore Roosevelt[188]

The "Lodge" Roosevelt referred to was his friend, the Republican Senator from Massachusetts, Henry Cabot Lodge. Roosevelt wrote on June 20, 1900 that "[Lodge] was my closest friend personally, politically and in every other way and occupied toward me a relationship that no other man has occupied or will occupy."[189]

Jacob Riis, also referred to, was an influential newspaper reporter, author, photographer and dedicated social reformer who had closely associated with TR while he was President of the board of Police Commissioners. The third man referenced, John R. Proctor, was a Democrat, and former Confederate soldier, from Kentucky who served on the Civil Service Commission after Hugh Thompson had left that office.

---

[188] Roosevelt, Theodore, *The Theodore Roosevelt Papers: Series 2: Letterpress Copybooks, -1916;* vol. 1, April 9-July 12. April 9, 1897, 1897. Manuscript/Mixed Material. https://loc.gov/item/ms382990319/. Library of Congress. Accessed June 10, 2024.

[189] Lodge, Henry Cabot, *Selections from the Correspondence of Theodore Roosevelt and Henry Cabot Lodge, 1884-1918*, volume 1 and volume 2, New York: Scribner's, 1925, p. 25.

Very clearly Roosevelt had the highest regard for Hugh Thompson to include only three men worthy to be on Thompson's "pedestal." For Roosevelt to have written to Hugh, spelling out his private feelings, man to man, in writing, is remarkable and very significant as a statement of their relationship. It is rare for men, despite strong personal bonds, to ever write in such terms.

Roosevelt's comment "I am sure you sympathized with my coming here. I have about done all I could in New York" refers to TR's resigning from the New York Police Commission, where he fought against entrenched corruption, and to accepting the appointment as Assistant Secretary of the Navy.

After Hugh Thompson joined New York Life, Theodore Roosevelt, now President, continued their personal correspondence. In one case a South Carolinian was seeking reappointment as a U.S. Marshal. Roosevelt sent a short personal letter, dated May 13, 1902, to Hugh Thompson at his New York Life office enclosing some letters about the reappointment commenting "how difficult it is to get at the facts." The President was, in a roundabout way, asking for Hugh's opinion on the reappointment. This example of Roosevelt's administrative style of soliciting the judgement of his friend for advice further illustrates the relationship between the two men. The content of the letters Roosevelt enclosed is unknown.

May 13, 1902

<u>*Personal*</u>

My Dear Governor Thompson

The enclosed letters, which please return to me as soon as you have read them, will give you an idea of how difficult it is to get at the facts concerning any public man.

Faithfully yours,
(signed) *Theodore Roosevelt*[190]

---

[190] Letter, May 13, 1902, from Theodore Roosevelt to Hugh S. Thompson. Theodore Roosevelt Papers. Library of Congress Manuscript Division. Theodore Roosevelt Digital Library, Dickinson State University.

Chapter 12
Southern Ties / Family Life

During the 1890s, while working as comptroller, Hugh Thompson's social life continued to be active. His children were growing up and getting married.

On December 13, 1892, Theodore Roosevelt, still a Civil Service Commissioner, wrote Hugh a handwritten personal letter. It is on 4x6 inch paper with a black mourning border around the edges, as he was still in mourning for the loss of his first wife and his mother in 1884. The envelope, also handwritten, is addressed to "Hon. H.S. Thompson, Comptroller N.Y. Life Insurance Co., Broadway, New York, N.Y." with no return address. It, too, has a black mourning border. The stamp has been torn off.

The letter datelined "Washington," reads:

Dear Governor Thompson,

We see by the papers that your daughter is engaged; is it true? If so pray accept our hearty congratulations and well wishes – though they are mainly due to the fortunate man.

Did you ever see my Cosmopolitan *article? If so, will you send it to our Irish friend*[191] *of the* News & Courier?

Cordially yours,

Theodore Roosevelt[192]

---

[191] Perhaps the "Irish friend" is in reference to the editor of the *News & Courier*, James C. Hemphill (1850-1927). He was born in South Carolina, not Ireland. Hemphill is a Scottish, not Irish, name.

[192] The December 13, 1892, letter from Theodore Roosevelt to HST is in the collection of Joan H. Clayton, Orlando, FL, 2024. The article Roosevelt mentioned in his letter was "A Colonial Survival," which appeared in the December 1892 (vol. XIV #2) issue of *The Cosmopolitan* on pages 229-

The daughter mentioned in TR's letter is Elizabeth Clarkson Thompson (1872-1942), named after her mother. She was known in the family and to friends as "Elise." She married a lawyer, James Greer Zachry (1857-1930), on February 14, 1893, at St. Thomas Church in New York. Her sister, Caroline Thompson (1874-1969), was maid of honor.[193]

Hugh Thompson was a member of the Confederate Veteran Camp of New York and would regularly attend their functions. He was present, along with a hundred other veterans, on January 19, 1893, at the annual banquet in celebration of the birthday of General Robert E. Lee. It is nearly certain that his wife, Elizabeth, was one of the many ladies of the veterans who were present. Twenty-eight-year-old Varina "Winnie" Davis, the youngest daughter of Confederate President Jefferson Davis, was a guest of honor. One of the speakers was the commander of the U.S. Grant Post, G.A.R. (Grand Army of the Republic, a Union veterans group).

Hugh Thompson spoke in response to the toast to "The Memory of Lee." While his exact words are not recorded, *The Baltimore Sun* newspaper reported Thompson

> *dwelt specially on the character of the great commander as a man. He touched on his career in the Mexican war as showing his ability as an executive officer. He reviewed his course at the opening of the civil war and his reasons for following the call for his services made by his native State [Virginia]. He briefly scanned the events of the war, calling to mind Lee's great magnanimity that prompted him always to give the praise of victory won to his generals, as an instance, the letter of congratulation to Stonewall Jackson after the battle of Chancellorsville – and to try and take to himself, even when not merited, the blame for defeat.*

---

236. The article praises the American spirit in warfare as well as in life over the rest of the world.

[193] *The National Tribune* (Washington, DC) December 22, 1892, p. 7. *Evening Star* (Washington, DC), December 24, 1892, p. 15. *Atlanta Journal* (Atlanta, GA), January 18, 1893.

General Lee's unselfishness in refusing the many brilliant posts held out to him after the war to devote himself to the education of the young men of the South was another notable evidence of this great character that inspired such love and confidence in the people of the South and made him their ideal soldier and leader.[194]

Eighteen-year-old Caroline Thompson, daughter of Hugh and Elizabeth, almost certainly attended this event, as well as other southern or Confederate themed occasions, along with her parents. Her lifelong admiration of General Lee is evidenced by her gift to her son, William H. Harrington (1912-1994), upon his graduation from Yale in 1935 with a degree in history, the newly published four-volume biography, *R.E. Lee*, by Douglas Southall Freeman.

The Thompsons were involved in clubs, organizations and social life wherever they lived. In the fall of 1894, a number of ladies formed the Wednesday Cotillion Association, alternatively known as The Southern Cotillion, which held events during the season. The association was modeled after the aristocratic St. Cecilia Society of Charleston and included an elaborate dinner along with the ball. Over a hundred couples would dance. *The New York Times* reported that the events were "attended by the most exclusive of the fashionable Southerners residing in this city." One of the patronesses of the organization was Elizabeth "Lieze" Thompson; another was Mrs. John A. McCall, wife of the President of the New York Life Insurance Company.

The December 13, 1894 Cotillion was attended by special guests, Mrs. Jefferson Davis and her daughter Winnie. Hugh Thompson was listed in the newspaper as one of the "other prominent people." The Thompsons' now 20-year-old daughter Caroline also attended. The January 9th Cotillion again included Mrs. Jefferson Davis, Winnie Davis and ex-governor of

---

[194] "Miss Davis Their Guest, Banquet and Speeches of the New York Confederate Veterans," *The Baltimore Sun* (Baltimore MD), January 20, 1893, p. 8.

Virginia, General Fitzhugh Lee, nephew of Gen. Robert E. Lee. The cotillion began about 1 a.m. and was led by a young man named George Toby and Caroline B. Thompson, the Thompson's daughter, which must have delighted her.[195]

Although not a member, Hugh Thompson attended the January 18, 1895, meeting and banquet of the Sons of the American Revolution. There were several speakers including a Major-General, an admiral, a Yale professor and others. Hugh Thompson spoke about the Revolutionary War battle of Cowpens.[196]

Hugh Thompson must have been impressed by the event and the SAR members, as six days later he applied for membership in the Sons of the American Revolution. He was accepted and given the State number 563 and National number 5363. He used his great grandfather, Captain James Williams, of the 10th Virginia Regiment as his qualifying ancestor. It is uncertain if that Captain James Williams of Virginia is indeed the same James Williams who died in Washington, Wilkes County, Georgia in 1794, who is known to be Hugh Thompson's great grandfather. However, Hugh Thompson did have another, confirmed, veteran in his great grandfather, Josiah Thompson, who was a Lieutenant in the Virginia Militia during the Revolutionary War.[197]

Shortly after the SAR meeting, the Thompsons took the train to Des Moines, Iowa for the New York Life Insurance Company convention.[198] Perhaps during the journey they spoke about how they had gone from South Carolina, to Washington, to New York and now were venturing into the vast mid-west,

---

[195] *The New York Times* (New York), December 13, 1894, p. 10, *The Sun* (New York), January 10, 1895, p. 7, *The New York Times* (New York), January 10, 1895, p. 9, *The Sun* (New York), January 31, 1895, p. 7.

[196] "Annual Banquet of the Sons of the American Revolution," *Buffalo Courier* (Buffalo, NY), January 5, 1895, p. 6.

[197] Josiah Thompson's wife, Mary Swann Thompson, was descended from Colonel Thomas Swann (1616-1680) of Jamestown, Virginia.

[198] "New York Life Convention," *Omaha Daily Bee* (Omaha, NE), February 6, 1895, p. 3.

which must have seemed a long way from their life in pre-war comfort and the post-war poverty of Columbia, South Carolina.

The Southern Relief Society held a charity ball on February 21, 1895, in Washington, DC. Always eager to help Southern or Confederate causes, Elizabeth "Lieze" Thompson, president of the New York chapter, attended.[199] The following night the Southern Society held a dinner in New York. The Thompsons may have been able to attend by travelling between the cities by train. Hugh Thompson was on the Executive Committee of the Society. New York Life's Chairman, Charles S. Fairchild, and President, John A. McCall, were present.[200] Two weeks later the Southern Society elected Hugh S. Thompson as vice-president.[201]

It may be hard to picture Elizabeth Thompson, the South Carolina lady, idling about the New Jersey shore, but apparently, she and her widowed sister, Maria Ellen "Nellie" Clarkson (1841-1929),[202] spent "several weeks" on the Jersey coast.[203]

The Thompsons were reported as staying at the famous Equinox House in Manchester, Vermont in August 1895.[204] It is unlikely that business or charity activities brought them there. It seems that they were simply enjoying a cool vacation at a beautiful location during the summer.

Elizabeth Thompson was prevented from acting as a patroness for the Wednesday Cotillion during the 1895-96 season as she was in mourning due to the death of her brother, John Ouldfield Heriot Clarkson, who died September 12th at the age of 57. The younger members of the family attended the dances, however.[205]

---

[199] *The Washington Times* (Washington, DC), February 10, 1895, p. 7.

[200] "For the Southern Society Dinner," *New York Tribune* (New York), February 22, 1895, p. 4.

[201] "Southern Society Officers," *The Philadelphia Inquirer* (Philadelphia, Pa), March 9, 1895, p. 4.

[202] After Maria Ellen "Nellie" Clarkson's marriage to Peter Bryce, she used the name "Ellen Peter Bryce".

[203] *The Montgomery Advertiser* (Montgomery, AL), July 28, 1895, p. 3.

[204] *The Burlington Free Press* (Burlington, VT), August 21, 1895, p. 6.

[205] "The Social World," *The New York Times* (New York), November 16, 1895, p. 8.

In April 1896, a benefit was held for the Confederate Veteran Camp of New York. It consisted of an extensive program of musical entertainment. A great many women were patronesses of the event including, of course, Elizabeth Thompson.[206]

At that time, many southern scholars believed that their history was not well preserved. It was thought that, in addition to the state historical societies, there was a need for a Southern Historical Association that would "have for its objects the encouragement of original research, discussion and conference among members, together with the widening of personal acquaintances, publication of work, and the collection of historical material."[207]

Education, and continuing education, were of vital interest to Hugh Thompson. He is listed among those "taking active interest in promoting the movement toward the establishment of the Southern Historical Association."[208] The organization took the name "Southern History Association." Hugh Thompson is listed in the January 1897 volume #1 on page 2 as a member. He again appears in 1899 volume III, page 156, indicating that he is a member of the Timrod Memorial Association. The Southern History Association never had more than 250 members and ceased to exist in 1907.

Hugh Thompson was a life-long Democrat. However, the Democratic Convention held in Chicago in July 1896 chose William Jennings Bryan as its candidate for President. Hugh Thompson disagreed with Bryan's fiscal policy. Bryan would travel the country speaking on his belief that the country should

---

[206] *New York Times* (New York), April 12, 1896, p. 20.

[207] "Southern Historians, The Necessity for Organizing an Association is Recognized, Eminent and Distinguished Men Who are Interested in the Formation of the Body," *Evening Star* (Washington, DC), April 24, 1896, p. 7.

[208] "Southern Historians, The Necessity for Organizing an Association is Recognized, Eminent and Distinguished Men Who are Interested in the Formation of the Body," *Evening Star* (Washington, DC), April 24, 1896, p. 7.

abandon the gold standard and substitute bimetallism, utilizing the price of gold and of silver.

Between 1893 and 1897 the country was in an economic "Panic." In the 19th century the term "Panic" was used instead of "Depression" used today. The economy was on the mind of every voter. The *New York Tribune*, July 22, 1896, carried an article "Hugh S. Thompson's Views." He is quoted as saying,

Speaking as an individual, I would say under no possible circumstances will I vote for Bryan or any other man on the platform adopted at Chicago. I believe that the election of Bryan would bring financial ruin as well as dishonor on this country. Any other than the gold standard would entail financial disaster to the country and to all its agricultural, commercial and industrial interests, by unsettling values, and would cause an enormous depreciation in all securities. Bimetallism for this country apart from the rest of the world would bring ruin and disgrace. International bimetallism, in my opinion, is visionary, and its accomplishment is too remote to be a factor in the consideration of the money question in this country as it is now presented to us.[209]

The *Courier-Journal* of Louisville, KY carried the same quote from Hugh Thompson under the headline "Will Not Vote for Bryan, Ex-Gov. Hugh S. Thompson Thinks Free Silver Means Ruin."[210]

The Republican candidate, William McKinley of Ohio, believed that the United States should remain committed to the gold standard. For many years Southerners had voted the straight Democratic ticket; it was their stronghold. However, in the election of 1896, a great many southerners and southerners living in the north, such as Hugh Thompson (Elizabeth, of course, could not vote and would die before women were

---

[209] "Hugh S. Thompson's Views," *New York Tribune* (New York), July 22, 1896, p. 3.

[210] "Will Not Vote for Bryan, Ex-Gov. Hugh S. Thompson Thinks Free Silver Means Ruin," *The Courier-Journal* (Louisville, KY), July 23, 1896, p.2.

allowed to vote) would for the first time in their lives vote for a Republican. He must have felt that his party, the party that he helped triumph in 1876, had abandoned him. He felt so strongly about the financial situation that he voted for McKinley. The *Wheeling Daily Intelligencer* wrote, "Hugh S. Thompson, comptroller of the New York Life Insurance Company, twice elected governor of South Carolina, and a life-long unswerving Democrat, is outspoken in his determination to vote for McKinley."[211]

Many Democrats of New York were dissatisfied with the Democratic Party. In December 1896, 125 prominent national Democrats, including Hugh Thompson, held a meeting in New York City to discuss the formation of a permanent organization to strengthen the national Democratic Party. It was suggested that a party be formed that would supersede the existing Democratic party. One speaker said, "We want an organization that will maintain the true principles of Democracy in the State and nation, so that the great mass of the voters will realize that we are right, and those who have gone away from our standard are wrong."

Hugh Thompson spoke in favor of the new party. "The South is a fruitful field for such a party as you propose to organize. It has been a question of races in the South, but I believe the time has come when we will vote for principle and not on account of races."[212]

While still interested in the politics and government of the U.S., Hugh Thompson's life increasingly revolved around family, social and historical activities.

An obelisk of New England granite, soaring 80 feet into the air, was dedicated in Mount Hope Cemetery in Hasting-on-Hudson, New York on May 22, 1897. This monument was dedicated by the New York Camp of Confederate Veterans. Trains brought a large number of people from New York

---

[211] "McKinley Gains, Southern Votes Heretofore Opposed to the Republicans, Leading Men Are Outspoken," *The Wheeling Daily Intelligencer* (Wheeling, WV), August 25, 1896.
[212] "Gold Democrats Active," *The Morning Times* (Washington, DC), December 4, 1896, p. 3.

including Hugh Thompson, who not only was a member of the New York Camp but also, as President, represented the contingent from The Southern Society. A procession was formed at the station to walk to the cemetery.

Led by a band playing Confederate as well as Union tunes, former Union soldiers, members of the Grand Army of the Republic, and other organizations of Union veterans were given the honor of leading the procession. Over twenty Union veteran organizations were represented. They were followed by 100 members of the Confederate Veterans camp and members of The Southern Society and the Sons of Confederate Veterans, as well as a large contingent of the Daughters of the Confederacy and ladies from branch organizations from Charleston, Richmond, Baltimore, and Nashville.

While Elizabeth Thompson was not mentioned in the newspaper accounts she undoubtedly was present as she was dedicated to the Confederate veteran causes. A daughter of Hugh Thompson's old Citadel classmate, former Confederate general and present Bishop of South Carolina, Ellison Capers, was present.[213] As Capers and Hugh Thompson were personal friends it may be that Capers' daughter accompanied Hugh and Elizabeth Thompson to the event.

A speaker, William Kelley, noted that the monument was consecrated by those once called "the enemy now known by the sweet name of brothers." The Confederate veteran commander accepted the monument and "spoke especially to the Union veterans expressing in warm and earnest words the appreciation by the Southern people and soldiers of generosity and kindliness of their former foes, dedicating the monument as a memorial, a pledge, and an expression of unending peace, union, and fraternity among Americans."[214]

---

[213] "To the Confederate Dead, Veterans of Both Armies United in Dedication of the Monument at Mount Hope Cemetery," *New York Times*, May 23, 1897.
[214] "To the Confederate Dead, Veterans of Both Armies United in Dedication of the Monument at Mount Hope Cemetery," *New York Times*, May 23, 1897.

Another speaker, one W.L. Wilson, a Confederate veteran and former Postmaster General, said that the monument, dedicated jointly by both the Union and Confederate veterans, was the fulfillment of the last prophecy and hope of General Grant. And, that the only rivalry in the future would be generous emulation in the performance of the duties of citizenship of a common country.

The monument bears the inscription "Sacred to the memory of the Heroic Dead of the Confederate Veteran Camp of New York" and on the opposite side,

> *Fold up the banners! Smelt the guns!*
> *Love rules, her gentler purpose runs.*
> *A mighty mother turns in tears,*
> *The pages of her battle years,*
> *Lamenting all her sons.*[215]

Strangely, this 1897 event reached out and touched Americans in 2017. In a remarkable twist of pre-conceived ideas, and great lack of historical knowledge of the origins of the monument, the town of Hastings-on-Hudson almost destroyed the monument. In August 2017, there were riots in Charlottesville, Virginia when a statue of Robert E. Lee was to be removed. Various organizations and individuals along the Hudson River thought that the monument in Mount Hope Cemetery represented honor for the Confederacy, hate, discrimination, promotion of slavery and white supremacy. The monument came within a whisker of being destroyed by unknowing people who did not realize just what this monument enshrined.

The monument, rather than promoting white supremacy, slavery, and hate, was in fact a demonstration, in stone, of reconciliation. Not only did many Union veterans participate in the dedication ceremony, but they also cared for the monument after it was erected. A chapter of the Sons of Union Veterans of

---

[215] "To the Confederate Dead, Veterans of Both Armies United in Dedication of the Monument at Mount Hope Cemetery," *New York Times*, May 23, 1897.

the Civil War conduct memorial services at the monument each April 27th – Confederate Memorial Day.

Paul Feiner, the town supervisor, and Peter Swiderski, the mayor, looked at the historical context and were instrumental in convincing the various parties that the monument was one of reconciliation. Feiner said, "today our country needs to stop hating. We all have to get along. We could learn a positive lesson from the men and women of 1897 who decided to put aside their past differences and be friends."[216] Hugh Thompson would have agreed with him completely.

Five years later, in June 1902, Hugh and Lieze Thompson returned to Mount Hope Cemetery for another memorial service hosted by the Confederate Veteran Camp of New York. A special train, from New York brought a couple hundred Confederate Veteran Camp and Daughters of the Confederacy members to Hastings-on-Hudson and returned them later in the afternoon. It was reported by the *New York Tribune* that photographs were taken.[217] This service may have been the last such outing for Hugh and Lieze Thompson.

The Confederate Veterans Camp of New York held its eighth annual banquet on the evening of January 22, 1898, in New York City. The occasion was given good coverage by *The New York Times*, which provides a glimpse of the proceedings.[218] About 200 members and guests including men belonging to the Sons of Confederate Veterans were present. The dining hall was decorated with large portraits of Generals R.E. Lee and Stonewall Jackson at the head of the table. United States and Confederate flags were draped there as well. It should be clarified that the "Confederate flag" was the

---

[216] *Greenville Daily Voice*, https://dailyvoice.com/new-york/greenburgh/news/confederate-monument-in-greenburgh-symbol-of-reconciliation-feiner-says/720638/ accessed June 21, 2024. https://westchestermagazine.com/life-style/is-the-mount-hope-obelisk-truly-a-confederate-memorial/ accessed June 21, 2024.

[217] *New York Tribune* (New York), Jun 2, 1902, p. 4. No photos have been located.

[218] "The Confederates Dine," *The New York Times* (New York), January 23, 1898, p. 9.

Confederate national flag and not the battle flag that most 21st century Americans consider the flag of the Confederacy. Small battle flags were among the more minor decorations.

The first toast, to "the President, Army, and Navy of the United States," was received "with loud cheering, the Southern yell being given with full effect, notwithstanding the age of many of those who joined in it and the long disuse of the special vocal exercise required to produce it. … The memory of Gen. Robert E. Lee, whose name was greeted with an apparently irrepressible storm of cheering when it was first mentioned, was drunk standing and in silence, while the bugle sounded 'taps.'"

An address was given on Stonewall Jackson by a Dr. McGuire who was Surgeon General on Jackson's staff during the war. In the course of his speech Dr. McGuire mentioned Rev. Dr. James P. Smith who was sitting at the commander's table. Smith covered Jackson's body with his own at the battle of Chancellorsville where Jackson was fatally wounded:

A rattle of applause at this quickly broke into a roar and then there was volley after volley of the screaming yell, as all the men present rose to their feet, waving napkins and handkerchiefs. Dr. Smith was forced to rise in his place and bow to repeated recognition of this tribute before Dr. McGuire could continue his speech.

After McGuire had finished speaking there was *another stirring incident of the evening when ex-Gov. Hugh S. Thompson, responding to the toast of "Albert Sydney Johnson" said that there was nothing of the sectional spirit in the honors paid by Southern men to their heroes, that Southerners would rally fast for defense of the common country, and that they had just pride in the fact that the most dangerous and difficult diplomatic duties now being performed for the country were in the hands of a gallant Confederate officer bearing the stainless name of Lee. The guests rose in one mass with one accord and cheered until they were hoarse.*[219]

Hugh Thompson was referring to former Confederate Major General Fitzhugh Lee (1835-1905), a nephew of R.E. Lee. Fitzhugh Lee was currently the consul-general of the United States to Havanna, Cuba. Tensions were high between the United States and the Spanish. In three weeks, the warship USS *Maine* would blow up in Havanna Harbor setting the stage for the onset of the Spanish American War.

A month later, on February 22, 1898, Hugh S. Thompson, as President of the Southern Society, presided over the annual dinner. The USS *Maine* had blown up the previous week. The New York newspapers *The Sun* and *New York Tribune* covered the dinner.[220] "The Air was full of patriotism" at the Hotel Savoy dinner meeting. "The banquet hall was draped with the Stars and Stripes and *America,* and *Star Spangled Banner* were sung with the same fervor as *Dixie.*"

In his opening address Hugh S. Thompson said, "It seems to be especially meet on this national holiday to pay our respects to the dead of the battleship Maine and to honor the living. The name of Sigsbee [Captain Charles D. Sigsbee, captain of the *Maine*] belongs in the list of American heroes, beside Jones, Decatur, Farragut, and all the others who have made famous the American sailor and soldier."

It is significant, with its unifying theme, for Hugh Thompson to have mentioned David Farragut, a southerner, who opposed secession and served in the U.S. Navy as a very successful rear admiral during the Civil War. Farragut is best known for his "Damn the torpedoes, full speed ahead" order at Mobile Bay.

---

[219] "The Confederates Dine," *The New York Times* (New York), January 23, 1898, p. 9.

[220] "Southern Society Dinner, the Speakers Refer to the Strained Relations with Spain," *The Sun* (New York), February 23, 1898, p. 3. "In True Southern Style, Loyal Celebration at the Savoy," *New York Tribune* (New York), February 23, 1898, p. 10.

Hugh Thompson continued, "Let us hope that the war cloud which seems to be gathering will be disrupted by the gentle breeze of peace, but if it is not to be, I know and you know that from the lakes to the Gulf, and from ocean to ocean, Americans will crowd one another in the rush to lay their gifts at the common altar of the country. Let us all hope though that peace will be vouchsafed to us." He then suggested a toast in memory of the dead of the *Maine*, which was drunk standing in silence.

The United States declared war on Spain on April 25, 1898. On May 6th Theodore Roosevelt resigned his position as Assistant Secretary of the Navy and received a commission as Lieutenant Colonel in the 1st United States Volunteer Cavalry, which would soon become known as the "Rough Riders." He would gain fame from his July 1st attack on San Juan Hill, in Cuba. With the war over, fame swept him to election as the Republican Governor of New York, an office he would hold until the end of 1900.

In June 1898, during the Spanish American War, a young Lieutenant, Victor Blue, from the battleship USS *Massachusetts* (BB-2) surreptitiously led a small scouting party ashore in Cuba to locate the Spanish fleet. He found the fleet in Santiago harbor and returned undetected to the USS *Massachusetts* to report. A few days later, using Lt. Blue's information, the United States fleet sank the Spanish fleet at the Battle of Santiago de Cuba.

An organization of women in South Carolina was formed to raise money for a gold medal for Lt. Blue. While born in North Carolina, Victor Blue grew up in South Carolina. On January 13, 1900, a ceremony took place on the afterdeck of the battleship USS *Massachusetts* in the Brooklyn Navy Yard.[221]

---

[221] The USS *Massachusetts* (BB2), commissioned in 1896, was the oldest battleship in existence. In 1920, at the end of its career, the 350-foot vessel was used as a target ship off the coast of Pensacola Florida. It was sunk in 26 feet of water by artillery fire 1.5 miles offshore. It is now a State of Florida Archaeological Preserve and artificial reef. It is a popular dive site. At low tide part of the superstructure breaks the surface. GPS 30 17.795' N, 87 18.720' W.

The officers and sailors were in formation as Captain Charles J. Train introduced Hugh Thompson who spoke a tribute to Lt. Blue's courage, then presented him with the gold medal from the ladies of South Carolina. The assembled men of the *Massachusetts* gave three cheers for Lt. Blue and three more for Hugh Thompson, who was accompanied by his wife, his daughters Caroline and Elizabeth Thompson Zachry, as well as his son John Means Thompson.[222]

In 1900 Hugh Thompson and Lieze were renting at 66 East 64th Street, New York City. With them, was their 28-year-old real estate broker son, Hugh S. Thompson, Jr. (1872-1917) and 25-year-old daughter, Caroline Beaumont Thompson (1874-1969). To make it even more of a family affair, the household included 27-year-old daughter Elizabeth "Elise" (1872-1942) and her 43-year-old husband James Greer Zachry (1857-1930), who was employed as a broker. There were also the Zachry children: Caroline (1894-1945), Elizabeth (1895-1943) and James Greer Zachry Jr (1900-1967).[223] Elizabeth "Elise" and James Greer Zachry had been married in New York in 1893.[224] It is unknown why the Zachrys would have been living with the Thompsons rather than a home of their own. To round out the household there were three female servants in residence.[225]

The meeting between Caroline, the eligible daughter of Hugh and Elizabeth "Lieze" Thompson, and her future husband, John Madison Harrington in the teeming metropolis of New York City was influenced by several forces acting in their favor. For one thing they both were Southerners. Surely, neither would consider marriage to anyone other than a Southerner. That limited the field of potential marriage partners considerably. However, there was the Southern Society.

---

[222] *New York Tribune* (New York), Jan. 14, 1900, p. 17.

[223] U.S. Census, 1900, June 7, 1900, City of New York.

[224] "Zachry-Thompson, A Notable Wedding in New York City Yesterday," *The Macon Telegraph* (Macon, GA), February 15, 1893, p. 1.

[225] One must wonder if Hugh and Lieze, now in their '60s, questioned if the kids would ever move out on their own.

The New York Southern Society, formed in 1886, was the largest, best known and best financed Southern regional organization in the North.[226] It admitted only men from the South or who had Southern ancestors.

Article Two of the Constitution of the New York Southern Society states:

> *The object of this Society is to promote friendly relations between Southern men residing or temporarily sojourning in New York City, and to cherish and perpetuate the memories and traditions of the Southern people.*[227]

The Society meetings were non-political and emphasized camaraderie of men of common backgrounds. The ideals of "Southern virtue and honor" as well as the "magic of the Southern past" and "superiority of the Southern people" were dominant themes. However, members swore loyalty to the "indissoluble union."[228] This was not a band of rebels or firebrands.

Hugh Thompson was a Life Member in the New York Southern Society. He had been a Vice President, President and served on the Executive Board. His son-in-law James Greer Zachry (husband of daughter, Elizabeth "Elise" Thompson) was also a member although less active.

Another member of the Southern Society was the young lawyer, John Madison Harrington (1874-1925), a Georgian who had graduated from the University of Georgia in 1894, where he was a member of Kappa Alpha fraternity and Phi Beta Kappa. He moved to New York where he graduated from New York

---

[226] Southerland, Donald E., "Southern Fraternal Organizations in the North," *Journal of Southern History*, vol. 53, no. 4 (Nov. 1987), p. 587-612.
[227] *Yearbook of the New York Southern Society*, for years 1901-1902, New York: Press of W.F. Vanden Houten, p. 52.
[228] Southerland, Donald E., "Southern Fraternal Organizations in the North," *Journal of Southern History*, vol. 53, no. 4 (Nov. 1987), p. 591, 597.

Law School in 1897.[229] He too would be elected Secretary, later Vice President, and then President of the Southern Society.

John M. Harrington, born in 1874, would not have been in the Civil War himself.[230] However, his father, William Henry Harrington (1846-1906), was a Confederate soldier. William was a cadet in the Georgia Military Institute and saw combat in 1864 and 1865.

Undoubtedly, John M. Harrington and Hugh Thompson would have met through the Southern Society. At the Society meeting of March 1, 1900, John M. Harrington was elected secretary.   The meeting was presided over by Hugh Thompson.[231] It would not be unusual if the men mentioned their hometowns. Hypothetically, perhaps on hearing that John Harrington was from West Point, Georgia, Hugh Thompson would comment that his son-in-law, James Greer Zachry, was from the same area. In response, John Harrington may have volunteered that his mother was Anna Zachry (1850-1887) and that James Greer Zachry would be his 3rd cousin. This may not have been how the first connection between Caroline Beaumont Thompson and John Madison Harrington was made, but it is plausible. Or, perhaps cousin James Greer Zachry may simply have contacted John Harrington and said that he was living in the household of Hugh Thompson and among the family was the

---

[229] "J.M. Harrington, Claim Lawyer, Dies, Long Noted as Authority on Land Litigation," *The Brooklyn Eagle* (Brooklyn, NY), September 18, 1925, p. 20. "J.M. Harrington Dies at Freeport, Nationally Known Attorney Was Only 50; an Author and Active in L.I. Civic Life," *Times Union* (Brooklyn, NY), September 18, 1925, p. 2.

[230] In June 1900, John M. Harrington was living as a lodger in an apartment house run by his uncle, Frederick Crane, at 117 West 13th Street, New York City. Uncle Fred was living there with his wife, John Harrington's aunt, Anna Lucille Harrington (1855-1935). She was a daughter of John Harrington's grandfather, John M. Harrington (1811-1865), and his wife Nancy Barrett (1815-1896). Other lodgers were John Harrington's brothers: 29-year-old Alfred Flournoy Harrington (1871-1929), a physician; 22-year-old Frank Trammell Harrington (1876-1945), a clerk; and 20-year-old William Henry Harrington (1882-1932), a clerk. [See U.S. Census, 1900, June 11, 1900, City of New York.]

[231] "Gift to The Southern Society," *New York Tribune* (New York, NY), March 2, 1900, p. 9.

charming daughter Caroline. We of the 21st century will never know for sure.

In addition to quarterly meetings, the organization also held annual dinners that were grand affairs at the Waldorf-Astoria. Women were invited to these annual dinners. The 17th Annual Dinner was held on February 21, 1903. The Dinner Committee for this occasion consisted of three men including both Hugh Thompson and John Harrington.[232]

In addition to the Southern Society, Hugh Thompson continued to be involved in other Southern preservation societies. On January 18, 1901, he attended the Confederate Veterans Camp dinner at the Waldorf-Astoria to commemorate the birthday of Robert E. Lee. The guest of honor was Mrs. Jefferson Davis, the widow of the former President of the Confederacy. Two hundred fifty people attended, half of them women. The first toast was to "The President and the Army and Navy of the United States; Invisible in peace, Invincible in War," which was drunk by all standing.[233]

In November 1900, Theodore Roosevelt was elected as William McKinley's Vice President. On September 6, 1901, McKinley was shot, and on September 14th he died. Theodore Roosevelt then became President at the age of 42. Fifty-six days later, on November 9, 1901, Hugh Thompson dined at the White House with his friend, now the President of the United States, Theodore Roosevelt. Roosevelt had him sent an invitation to which Hugh replied by telegram to Roosevelt's secretary, "I accept with pleasure the President's invitation to dine with him tomorrow at seven thirty."[234] As dinner at the White House was an honor, one may assume the dinner invitation included Elizabeth and Caroline. Only Hugh Thompson's brief reply telegram of acceptance remains to record the event.

---

[232] *Yearbook of the New York Southern Society,* for years 1901-1902, New York: Press of W.F. Vanden Houten, p. 11.

[233] *New York Tribune* (New York), Jan. 19, 1901, p. 6.

[234] The one-line telegram is part of the collection at The Theodore Roosevelt Center at Dickinson State University. It is available online. The reply telegram was sent to George B. Cortelyou, Roosevelt's secretary. Theodore Roosevelt Papers. Library of Congress Manuscript Division.

The following year Hugh, and almost certainly Elizabeth and Caroline, were present at the annual dinner of the New York Confederate camp when the guest of honor was Robert E. Lee's daughter, Miss Mary Custis Lee. Mrs. Jefferson Davis was also present. President Theodore Roosevelt, sent his regrets writing,

It was once my good fortune to speak to the Southern Society in New York and I enjoyed it so much that I wish it were now possible to be present at the reunion of the Confederate camp, but I find it to be utterly out of the question. It is a double regret to have to refuse you as well as to lose the pleasure of being present at the camp. Give my most cordial good wishes to the members of the camp and their guests, and believe me, hoping that the reunion may be most successful.[235]

On April 9, 1902, President Roosevelt, at a banquet given in his honor at the Charleston Hotel, [200 Meeting Street, torn down in 1960] responded to the first toast of the evening with a tribute to Hugh Thompson saying,

And now a word to you of Charleston and South Carolina. Just twelve years ago when I first went to Washington to take part in governmental work I was immediately thrown into singularly close contact and intimacy with a South Carolinian. It was my good fortune to work with him for three years, and for the nine years since and for as long as I shall continue to be in public life, it will be to me ever a spur to try to do my whole duty to the Republic because I have been thrown intimately in contact with as fair and as high-minded a public servant as this country has ever had, my old friend, your former Governor, Hugh Thompson.[236]

This was Hugh Thompson's last public appearance in South Carolina.

---

[235] *New York Tribune* (New York), Jan. 21, 1902, p. 5.

[236] *The State* (Columbia, SC), November 21, 1904, p. 6. Thompson, Henry T., *The Establishment of the Public School System.* 60.

On April 13, 1902, Hugh Thompson was a pallbearer at the funeral of Wade Hampton in Columbia, SC. General, and later Governor, Hampton was buried at Trinity Church. Twenty thousand people attended the funeral.[237]

In 1904, now 68 years old, Hugh Thompson was slowing down. He was still actively involved with New York Life Insurance Company, but his public appearances were greatly reduced. He was stricken with influenza in March of 1904 from which he never recovered. He also suffered from chronic asthma.

President Roosevelt sent Hugh Thompson a letter, November 4, 1904. It is typed with a handwritten signature:

My dear Governor Thompson,

I have just learned that you were a little under the weather this fall, and, my dear fellow, I write to say how concerned I am that you should have had any trouble at all, and how pleased I am now to learn that your health is mending.

Give my warm regards to Mrs. Thompson. I think of you both often, and always with the most affectional regards

Faithfully yours,

(signed) Theodore Roosevelt[238]

Roosevelt probably knew that Hugh's health was not "mending" but wanted to cheer him. When it was apparent that Hugh was not going to recover and was sinking, the family sat by his bedside in turns. On the night of November 18th or 19th his son, Thomas Clarkson Thompson, was sitting with him. Hugh asked to see a letter from President Theodore Roosevelt that had arrived that day. Thomas wrote that

> *the letter was a very cordial invitation to my mother and father to visit the White House and renew the old Civil Service days. My father requested that I read it to him again. It seemed to touch him very much. He was*

---

[237] "Wade Hampton's Funeral, Imposing Demonstration Participated in by More than 20,000 Mourners," *The New York Times*, April 14, 1902.

[238] Letter: T. Roosevelt to H.S. Thompson, November 4, 1904. Digital Library, Theodore Roosevelt Center at Dickinson State University.

exceedingly fond of Roosevelt and Roosevelt always treated him with every courtesy and consideration. Seeing that he was wide awake, I said to him, "Father is Roosevelt an honest man?" He looked at me very intently for a moment and said, "Incorruptibly so, my son, but no one ever talked as much as Roosevelt does and sticks strictly to the truth."[239]

[239] Thompson, Thomas Clarkson, *The Narratives of Thomas Clarkson Thompson, 1860-1938*, edited and annotated by H. T. Harrington, 31. The letter from Roosevelt has not survived.

Chapter 13
An Honorable End

Hugh S. Thompson died at 9 pm November 20, 1904, at his home at 34 East 53rd Street in New York at the age of 68. His body was taken by train to Columbia, South Carolina, where it lay in state in the State House building. The flag on the State House was flown at half-staff. Newspapers all over the country carried obituaries covering his death and career.

He was buried on Wednesday, November 23 at Trinity church where he had been married and been a member of the vestry. The church is located across the street from the Statehouse where so many dramatic events of his life took place. His tombstone is of granite and stands in the Thompson lot, along with other family members, very close to the north side of the church building.

The service at Trinity Church was conducted by Bishop Ellison Capers, who had been a cadet with Hugh for three years at The Citadel. The officers of New York Life Insurance Company were in the funeral procession, including Jonathan A. McCall, president, D.P. Kingsley, first vice president, E.D. Randolph, treasurer, S.M. Ballard, secretary, and S.O. Vanderpace, medical director.

Officers of the State of South Carolina came next: Governor Heyward, Chief Justice Y.J. Pope, Associate Justices Woods and Gary, Lieut. Governor Sloan, Secretary of State Gantt, Comptroller General Jones, General John D. Frost, Attorney General Gunter, Assistant Attorney General Townsend, Superintendent of Education Martin and others. Then came Col. John P. Thomas and alumni of The Citadel.

The Governor's Guard, of which Hugh Thompson was a member, was represented by a detail. A large group representing Camp Hampton of the United Confederate Veterans attended. As Hugh Thompson was a member of the Richland Lodge no. 39, the Masons were also represented, as was The Southern Society and the New York Confederate Veterans Camp.

Carnations were sent by President Roosevelt, and his wife, Edith Roosevelt, sent roses. These were placed on the casket. A six-foot-tall floral cross was sent by the executive officers of New York Life, which was made by the J.M. Connelley Company of Charleston and "was one of the most exquisite floral offerings ever seen here."

At the time of Hugh S. Thompson's death, President Roosevelt sent a telegram to the family:

> *Pray accept my profound sympathy for you and your mother in your great bereavement. I cannot say how distressed I am at the death of your father. I never met a braver, gentler, or more upright man.*[240]

Mrs. Roosevelt also sent her condolences in a letter to Mrs. Hugh S. Thompson.

First page of condolence letter from Edith Kermit Roosevelt

---

[240] "Governor Thompson to be Buried Today," *The State* (Columbia, SC), November 23, 1904, p. 8.

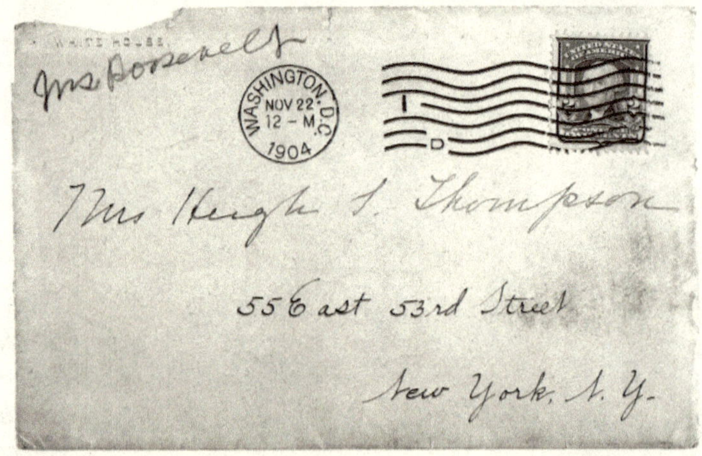

Hugh Thompson belonged to The Century and Reform
Clubs, the Confederate Veterans' Association, New York
Alumni Association of Alpha Tau Omega Fraternity, the
Masons, and the Southern Society, of which he was President

and had served in other positions.[241] The University of South Carolina honored Hugh Thompson prior to his death by granting him an honorary LL.D. degree in 1900.

He was survived by his wife of 46 years, Elizabeth Clarkson Thompson; his sons: Colonel Henry Tazewell Thompson who was Lt. Col. of the 2nd South Carolina Regiment in the Spanish American War; Thomas Clarkson Thompson of Chattanooga who was one of the most prominent insurance men in the South; John Means Thompson, a real estate broker in New York City; Waddy Thompson, a historian of Atlanta; Hugh Smith Thompson, Jr., a real estate broker in New York City; his daughters: Elizabeth Clarkson Thompson, wife of James G. Zachry, a broker in New York City; and Caroline Beaumont Thompson who lived with her parents in New York.

One of the finest tributes to Hugh S. Thompson was written not by a President of an Insurance Company or even the President of the United States. It was written by a young man at the St. Louis, Missouri office of New York Life. His signature is difficult to read but may be Harry Sorean or Harry S. Orean. The letter, dated November 17, 1904, is addressed to John A. McCall, President New York Life.

Dear Mr. McCall

It was with a feeling of sadness that I read in last evening's paper an account of the serious illness of our Comptroller, Mr. Thompson, and while I have never had the pleasure of meeting Gov. Thompson personally I have had so much correspondence with him as Cashier of the Missouri Clearing House that I feel as though he were my friend, as I believe he has been a friend of every young Cashier.

In all of the hundreds of letters received from Mr. Thompson, as Comptroller, never has there been one

---

[241] A great many obituaries appeared across the country. Information about the funeral was obtained through the articles appearing in *The New York Times, The Herald, The Sun, The American, The Daily News, The Press,* excellent coverage in *The News and Courier* (Charleston), *Macon Telegraph* (Macon, Georgia), *Richmond News Leader.*

This letter was written on a Thursday. Hugh Thompson died on Sunday the 20th. Therefore, it seems unlikely that this tribute reached him in time.

Hugh Thompson left his estate, valued at $8,000, to his wife, "Lize C. Thompson."

Hugh S. Thompson's death certificate contains an error. It lists "Elizabeth Clarkson," as his mother instead of his wife. Hopefully, that won't cause too many problems down through the ages. His cause of death is difficult to read but in part he died of emphysema, arterial sclerosis, chronic nephritides,[243] and pulmonary edema. He was living at 34 East 53rd Street.

---

[242] Copy of original letter on New York Life Insurance letterhead, in possession of Hugh T. Harrington, Gainesville, GA, 2024.
[243] Nephritides is a condition where the kidneys become inflamed and inadequately filter waste from the blood.

Chapter 14
Elizabeth Anderson Clarkson Thompson

Regrettably, there is little hard evidence about the life of Elizabeth "Lieze" Thompson. That, of course, is no fault of her own as she lived in an era when a woman expected to only appear in the newspapers when she was married and when she died.

Lieze was born in the old Clarkson family home, originally owned by her grandfather, William Clarkson (1760-1825), at 18 Bull Street, Charleston, South Carolina, April 19, 1840. She was the 6th child of 14 born to Thomas Boston Clarkson (1809-1879) and Sarah Caroline Heriot (1807-1877). All 14 children lived: the last, Sophia Johnston Clarkson (1849-1855), being born Christmas Day 1849 when her mother, Sarah Caroline Heriot Clarkson, was 42.

Lieze had 13 children, but only 9 lived long enough to be named. Caroline Beaumont Thompson (1874-1969) was the last child born to survive. She would outlive her last sibling by 27 years.

As we have seen Lieze was a strong supporter of the Confederacy. After the war she supported the memory and veterans of the Confederacy. She also stood behind her husband throughout his career. Hers was the charm, grace and quiet strength of a time that Margaret Mitchell described as gone with the wind.

Her son, Thomas Clarkson Thompson (1860-1938), wrote, when discussing Reconstruction,

I do not intend in this paper to stress the ordeal through which my mother and father were forced to pass but I do want my children and grandchildren to know that I never saw my mother out of humor unless somebody interfered with her children. My father was often inclined to be despondent, but I can recall as a little boy in the sparsely

*furnished sitting room the cheerful conversation of my
mother and her friends. She always had friends and was
the most beloved person I have ever known.*[244]

She died suddenly at the home of her daughter, Elizabeth
the wife of James Greer Zachry, 68 East 83rd Street, New York
City. Her obituaries were short and to the point with little
extraneous information.

However, the obituary appearing in the Columbia, South
Carolina newspaper, *The State*, appears to have been written by
someone who knew Lieze, despite her not having lived in
Columbia for over 20 years. Along with the usual details of
survivors and burial plans, a personal paragraph was included:

*This announcement will be received with sincere sorrow
by a large circle of friends throughout the State, for Mrs.
Thompson was a lady of unusual personal magnetism.
Her friends were not confined to this city, where her
home and that of her distinguished husband was graced
by their genial manners.*[245]

"Personal magnetism" and "genial manners" are terms that
seem to define her and go along with her son's comment that she
"always had friends and was the most beloved person I have
ever known."

Elizabeth Clarkson Thompson's death certificate indicates
she died of acute dilation of the heart, as well as something
illegible that is listed as "non-traumatic." She is recorded as
having lived at 68 East 83rd St., New York City. She was buried
at Trinity Church in Columbia, South Carolina.

On January 29, 1892, she had applied for membership in
the Daughters of the American Revolution. She used her
descent from militia colonel Robert Heriot of South Carolina as
her qualifying ancestor. Her National DAR number is 1160.

---

[244] Thompson, Thomas Clarkson, *The Narratives of Thomas Clarkson
Thompson, 1860-1938*, edited and annotated by H. T. Harrington, 3.
[245] *The State* (Columbia, SC), July 9, 1909.

Lieze Thompson was also Vice President of the United Daughters of the Confederacy in 1908.[246]

In 1985, this author asked a friend who was interested in handwriting analysis to give impressions of Lieze's handwriting. The handwriting sample was the DAR application. The page indicating that she was the wife of an ex-governor was not included in the sample as it was thought it might influence the results.

The handwriting analyst provided the following traits or descriptions of Lieze Thompson, as she understood them to be, from examining the handwriting: "attention to detail, active woman, good mind, analytic imagination, initiative, jealous, doer rather than planner, involved in many activities, restless nature, very enthusiastic, strong will, determined, temper if thwarted, lots of drive and determination, argumentative, fluidity of thought, independent ideas, pride/dignity in actions and accomplishments, stubborn, possessive of what is hers."

It is wished that more, a lot more, was known about this remarkable woman. If she had only kept a daily journal of her life experiences. What a story that would be. Perhaps, forgotten in some attic of a descendant...

---

[246] *The New York Times* (New York, NY), November 8, 1908, p. 50.

Epilogue

Henry T. Thompson donated a portrait of his father, painted in Washington by Williams Welch in 1881, to the State of South Carolina. On January 26, 1906, this portrait was presented to the House of Representatives of the General Assembly by Governor D.C. Heyward saying, "it is my great privilege to entrust to your care this portrait of one, who in life, craved no greater honor than to serve his State nobly and well – and this honor was his."[247] The portrait is no longer listed among those held at the State House. Its current location is unknown.

Two years after Hugh Thompson's death, his daughter Caroline Beaumont Thompson (1874-1969) married John Madison Harrington. [248] The wedding took place at St. Michael's Church in Charleston, South Carolina on December 27, 1906. The wedding ceremony was performed by Hugh Thompson's old friend and Citadel comrade, the Bishop of South Carolina, Ellison Capers. He was assisted by Rev. John Kershaw, rector of St. Michaels.

Despite the death of his friend, Teddy Roosevelt's concern with the family was not over. He appointed a grandson of Hugh and Elizabeth Thompson to West Point. Roosevelt wrote Elizabeth "I am only too glad to hear from you at any time and to do anything I can for you. You know what pleasure I took in appointing your grandson to West Point."[249] The grandson was

---

[247] *Journal of the House of Representatives of the General Assembly of the State of South Carolina*, Columbia: State Printers, 1906, p. 294.

[248] Information on the wedding is from Caroline's "The Bride, Her Book" (wedding gift from Archibald Orme Harrington) containing autographs, clippings, long list of gifts, telegrams and various information regarding the wedding. The Bride's Book is in the possession of Joan H. Clayton, Orlando FL., 2024. Also, *Evening Post* (Charleston, SC), December 29, 1906, p. 6.

[249] Letter Theodore Roosevelt to Elizabeth Anderson Clarkson Thompson, November 24, 1908. Theodore Roosevelt Papers. Library of Congress

Thomas Clarkson Thompson, Jr., son of Hugh and Elizabeth's first son, Thomas Clarkson Thompson. Roosevelt's connection with young Tom Thompson goes back at least to 1902 when Roosevelt was in Chattanooga to give a speech. Twelve-year-old Tom was at the auditorium to see and hear the President. As Tom filed into the room Roosevelt called to him and they spoke briefly. The newspaper commented that "the Thompsons and the Roosevelts are old friends."

The President inquired of Tom about the health of his grandmother Elizabeth, Hugh Thompson's wife. He had heard that she was ill and taking the sulfur waters at Richfield Springs, New York.

When asked what his intentions were, young Tom said, "I am going to work for West Point, Mr. President." The President replied, "that's right, Tom, and if I have any influence, you shall have the appointment."

Quick on his feet, Tom replied, "thank you, Sir: but if I don't get the appointment I am going to enlist." That response brought a "great laugh" from the President who commented, "That's right, young man, that's the proper American spirit." The President then waived in goodbye and said, "I won't forget my promise."[250] What a day that must have been for young Tom Clarkson.

This interaction raises questions regarding just how much contact there was between Hugh Thompson and his friend President Roosevelt. How did the President know, or recognize, young Tom Thompson and how did he know about Elizabeth being at Richfield Springs. The inference is that the Thompsons, even after Hugh's death, and the President were closer and in more frequent communication than can be gleaned from the newspapers. Regrettably, no personal papers from Hugh Thompson, or Elizabeth, have survived.

The children and grandchildren of the Thompson family arranged for two stained glass windows to be created in memory

---

Manuscript Division. Theodore Roosevelt Digital Library. Dickinson State University.
[250] *The Daily Times*, Chattanooga, Tennessee, September 9, 1902, p. 2.

of Hugh S. Thompson and his wife Elizabeth C. Thompson and to be placed in Trinity Episcopal church, now Cathedral. On Sunday, January 26, 1913, a short ceremony was conducted by the bishop of the diocese, after the regular service. The windows, located in the baptistry, are almost directly above the Thompson graves on the north side of the churchyard. The

windows depict "'The Presentation of Christ in the Temple' described by St. Luke, chapter 1, verses 22-39. It is executed in very rich and yet subdued tints of the finest antique glass by Mayer & Co., at their studios in Munich, Bavaria, Germany, after a design by Prof. Blaim of the Munich academy."[251]

The following day, at the site of the Columbia Male Academy, on the Northeast corner of Laurel and Pickens Streets in Columbia, South Carolina, was an unveiling of a stone bearing a plaque stating, "On this site stood The Columbia Male Academy. Here was conducted Thompson's School from 1865 to 1880 by Hugh S. Thompson in whose

---

[251] "Bronze Tablet Was Unveiled," *The Columbia Record* (Columbia, SC), January 27, 1913, p. 6.

memory this tablet is erected by his grateful pupils."[252] The stone and plaque regrettably are long gone.

It was quite an event. The Columbia newspaper, *The State*, devoted two entire pages to the history and career of Hugh S. Thompson, as well as reminiscences and tributes written by former students and faculty.[253] This is remarkable in that he had been dead for eight years and had not been principal of the school for twenty-eight years.

The program for the unveiling of the plaque took place at noon on January 29, 1913. The invocation was delivered by Reverend Kirkman G. Finlay. That was followed by the audience singing of *America*. Introductory remarks were made by Melvin D. Kirk, President of the Alumni Association of Thompson's School. *Auld Lang Syne* was then sung by the audience. During the singing of *Auld Lang Syne* the tablet was unveiled.[254]

The audience then moved on to the auditorium of Taylor School where they sang Henry Timrod's *Carolina*. John Peyre Thomas gave the address. It will be remembered that John Peyre Thomas was a member of the Citadel class of 1851, English professor, Superintendent of the Arsenal Academy, and Captain of Company B and led the Arsenal cadets in combat at Tulifinny Creek while Captain Hugh Thompson commanded Company A, The Citadel cadets. When The Citadel reopened in 1882, he was named Superintendent; he was also a member of the Board of Visitors and named State Historian in 1887. Very regrettably, no text of that address survives. After John Thomas, the program was closed with a benediction given by Reverend Charles E. Burts.

---

[252] Thompson, Henry T., *The Establishment of the Public School System*. 61. Copy of 1913 unveiling ceremony program in collection of Hugh T. Harrington, Gainesville, GA., 2024. The printed program "Public Exercises held at the Taylor School, Columbia. S.C. on the occasion of The Unveiling of the Tablet, Wednesday, January 29th, 1923" curiously bears the wrong day and date. The events took place on Monday, January 27, 1913.
[253] *The State* (Columbia, SC), January 267, 1913, p. 26-27.
[254] Program of the *Public Exercises held at the Taylor School, Columbia, S.C. on the occasion of the Unveiling of the Tablet, Wednesday, January 29, 1913*. Collection of Joan Harrington Clayton, Orlando, FL.

An attendee at the unveiling event, Edward S. Joynes of Columbia, wrote a letter to the editor of *The State*:

> *It was a remarkable, indeed, a unique occasion. It is not remarkable that a family of noble sons and daughters should honor the memory of a noble father. It is not strange that a large crowd should gather to honor the memory of one who has held, and honored, the highest offices of State, and of public trust outside of the State. The remarkable fact was that it was none of these high offices that this extraordinary gathering sought to honor. It was not the State superintendent of education, not the brilliant governor, not the assistant secretary of the treasury, not the civil service commissioner honored by two presidents, not the great financier, who controlled millions of money – not any nor all of these, though all were deserving of honor – but it was Hugh S. Thompson, the schoolmaster, in whose memory was gathered this remarkable assembly, with a unity and depth of grateful veneration such as I have rarely elsewhere witnessed.*
>
> *What did it mean – what the explanation of this wide and profound sentiment, after so many years? There have been other good schools and schoolmasters, then why this remarkable demonstration? The answer is, that Hugh Thompson – in the ruin and desolation of the South – in personal poverty and obscurity, clearly grasped the idea that the only salvation of the State is in the education of the people. Conditions were profoundly depressing and discouraging; poverty stared him in the face; but under such conditions he founded and built a school and performed a work which, I make bold to say – without belittling his later services – was his greatest service and his chief claim to the gratitude of posterity. The benefit of his work and of his example in Columbia and in South Carolina at that time was and is incalculable. Like another great teacher – with whom it was my privilege once to serve – he founded his school on two great principles only – honor and obedience – the honor of personal life, and obedience to law – the*

supreme tests of the good man and good citizen, and these principles he illustrated in his own life and by precept and example, instilled into his pupils, at a time when such lessons were supremely needed. Therefore, not forgetting the public official and my later friend, to whom I owe so much, I take off my hat, most devoutly, to Hugh Thompson, the schoolmaster.

The same lessons are needed today by our people, under conditions hardly less critical than those of 1865, when Thompson began his work. Now, as then, the safety of the state lies in the education of the people. May the statesmen of this day, with their wider experience and greater opportunity, realize, as he did, this great truth. Then may they, too, learn, as he did, that "The Path of duty is the way to Glory."[255]

One Alfred Hampton of Galveston, Texas wrote,

...the alumni of the famous Thompson school are about to give tardy recognition to the memory of one of South Carolina's greatest men, our lamented and beloved friend and teacher, Capt. Hugh S. Thompson, whose example and teachings have been an inspiration for a life of rectitude to the hundreds who were so fortunate as to have attended said institution of learning.

Never will I forget a circumstance one of many vividly impressed upon my mind, which is typically illustrative of the character of the man. One day an old black mammy was passing in front of the Thompson school when some of our thoughtless boys indulged in careless jests at her expense, which no sooner came to the notice of our stern disciplinarian, but true, kind and courteous friend, Capt. Thompson, than he immediately summoned all the boys into the main school room and, standing erect, his eyes flashing, and his wonderfully handsome face plainly showing his earnestness and his displeasure, he delivered a lecture in that melodiously

---

[255] "Honor to Schoolmaster," *The State* (Columbia, SC), January 31, 1913.

stirring voice of his, impressing upon us the fact that every human being, whether black or white, whether poor or rich, is entitled to that courteous treatment which is indicative of a true heart and a manly nature.

Undoubtedly many of the old boys will recall the circumstances, as I am confident no one who listened to that talk straight from the shoulder will ever forget the lesson taught thereby.[256]

Hugh Thompson was honored on November 3, 1962, with a portrait, which hangs in The Citadel's Memorial Library.

The modern South Carolina Department of Education summed up Hugh S. Thompson's work and achievements:

Hugh S. Thompson is known as the father of South Carolina's modern public school system and the only professional educator to serve as governor. He laid the foundations for the development of the state's public school system. As superintendent, he helped win passage of the 1878 school system law that centralized management of the school system in a state board of commissioners. He worked to equalize expenditures for white and Black schools, established summer teachers' institutes in 1880, and was responsible for the creation of the State Teacher's Association in 1881. His greatest achievement was winning mass support for public education and support for Blacks, in particular, against a tradition of public hostility, apathy, and prejudice.

He also believed that it was extremely necessary for South Carolina to have well-trained teachers. He emphasized that in no other profession did people try to practice without training, and he reminded his supporters that teaching was one of the finest professions in the world.

Thompson continued his advocacy of educational improvement, support for civil service and tax reform,

---

[256] "Thompson School Reunion Will Be a Great Success," *The State* (Columbia, SC), January 12, 1913, p. 11.

and called for a rigid economy in government. He was appointed assistant secretary of the U.S. Treasury by President Grover Cleveland on June 28, 1886 and resigned the governorship on July 10.

Thompson served as principal of the Columbia Male Academy from 1865 until 1880. During his tenure, he forged the institution into one of the state's premier preparatory schools and it became universally known as "Thompson's school."[257]

After all his achievements are weighed, Hugh S. Thompson's greatest accomplishments, and even his reason for being, was his work in education. As in Roosevelt's "The Man in the Arena," it was Hugh Thompson who "knows in the end the triumph of high achievement."

---

[257] South Carolina Department of Education, https://ed.sc.gov/newsroom/former-state-superintendents-of-education/hugh-s-thompson/ accessed May 3, 2024.

Appendix
Hugh Smith Thompson - Chronology

1836, Jan. 24	Hugh S. Thompson is born	Charleston, SC.
1840, Apr. 19	Elizabeth "Lieze" Anderson Clarkson is born	18 Bull St., Charleston, SC.
1856	Graduated from The Citadel	Charleston, SC.
1857	Assistant Teacher, Columbia Male Academy	Columbia, SC.
1858	Appointed Assistant Professor of French in the Arsenal Academy, Columbia. Rank of 2nd Lt.	Columbia, SC.
1858 Apr. 6	Married Elizabeth Anderson "Lieze" Clarkson at Trinity Episcopal Church	Columbia, SC.
1859	Promoted to 1st Lieutenant, Arsenal Academy	Columbia, SC.
1859 July 6	Son, Henry Tazewell Thompson, born	Columbia, SC.
1860 Sep. 21	Son, Thomas Clarkson Thompson, born	Columbia, SC.
1861 Aug. 28	Board of Visitors of The SC Military Academy promoted Hugh S. Thompson to Captain and transferred him to The Citadel Academy as Professor of Belles-Lettres and Ethics	Columbia, SC.
1863	Wife, Lieze, moves from Charleston to Columbia for safety	Columbia, SC.
1863 Jan. 21	Daughter, Elizabeth Anderson Thompson, born	Columbia, SC.
1863 Sept. 7	Daughter, Elizabeth Anderson Thompson, died	Greenville, SC.
1864 June 14	Son, John Means Thompson, born	Columbia, SC.

Date	Event	Location
1864 Dec. 7	Capt. of Citadel Cadets at Battle of Tulifinny Creek	SC.
1865 Feb. 17	Columbia, SC burn by General Sherman. Hugh S. Thompson, sick with typhoid and unable to walk, is taken to Greenville. His wife, Elizabeth Clarkson Thompson, also flees ahead of Sherman's forces	Columbia and Greenville, SC.
1865-1880	Principal, Columbia Male Academy - aka Thompson's School	Columbia, SC.
1866	Daughter, Eliza Cornelia Thompson, born	Columbia, SC.
1866 Nov. 1	Hugh S. Thompson's father, Henry Tazewell Thompson, dies at the age of 54	Greenville, SC.
1867 Aug. 13	Son, Waddy Thompson, born	Columbia, SC.
1872 Jan. 19	Son, Hugh Smith Thompson, born	Columbia, SC.
1872 Dec. 5	Daughter, Elizabeth Clarkson "Elise" Thompson, born	Columbia, SC.
1873 May 10	Hugh S. Thompson's mother, Agnes Smith Thompson, dies age 57	Charleston, SC.
1874 June 10	Daughter, Caroline Beaumont Thompson, 1874-1969, born	Columbia, SC.
1876-1882	State Superintendent of Education of South Carolina	Columbia, SC.
1882-1884	Governor of South Carolina, 1st term.	Columbia, SC.
1884 Mar. 4	Daughter Eliza Cornelia burned when dress caught fire from fireplace at Governor's Mansion	Columbia, SC.
1884 Mar. 15	Daughter Eliza Cornelia died from lockjaw as a result of burns	Columbia, SC.
1884-1886	Governor of South Carolina, 2nd term	Columbia, SC.

1886 July 10	Resigned from Governor to become Assistant Secretary of US Treasury	Washington, DC
1886-1889	Assistant Secretary of US Treasury	Washington, DC
1889-1892	United States Civil Service Commissioner; resigned May 15, 1892	Washington, DC
1890 Jan. 14, 28, and Feb. 11	President and Mrs. Harrison invited Hugh Thompson "and the ladies of his family" to meet "the Diplomatic Corps," to a "Reception to the Congress and the Judiciary," and "to meet the Officers of the Army and Navy and Marine Corps."	Washington, DC
1892-1904	Comptroller, New York Life Insurance Company	New York, NY
1896 Feb. 1	Elected to membership in The Century Association in New York. His membership was proposed by Theodore Roosevelt and seconded by Edward Cary	New York, NY
1900	Received the degree of LL.D. from the University of South Carolina	Columbia, SC.
1901 Nov. 9	Dinner with President Theodore Roosevelt at the White House	Washington, DC
1902 Apr. 13	Pallbearer at funeral of Wade Hampton	Columbia, SC.
1904 Nov. 20	Hugh S. Thompson died	34 E. 53rd St. New York City
1906 Jan. 26	A portrait of Hugh S. Thompson was presented to the SC General Assembly by Governor D.C. Heyward. The portrait was a gift from Col. Henry T. Thompson, a son of Hugh S. Thompson	Columbia, SC.

1913 Jan. 29	Tablet commemorating Columbia Male Academy, Thompson's School, by his former students	Unveiled on Laurel Street, Columbia, SC.
1962 Nov. 3	Portrait of Hugh S. Thompson unveiled at The Daniel Library, the main library of The Citadel	Charleston, SC.

Annotated Bibliography

<u>Books</u>

Baker, Gary, *Cadets in Gray*. Columbia, SC, Palmetto Bookworks, 1989.

Bond, O.J., Colonel, *The Story of The Citadel*. Richmond, VA, Garrett and Massie, 1936.
Includes Coffin, George M., "My Recollection of Fight at Tulifinny Creek, South Carolina, in December, 1864," 1929. Also included, report of The Citadel commander, Major James B. White. Reprint, Southern Historical Press, Greenville, SC, 1989.

Harrington, Hugh T., *More Milledgeville Memories*. Charleston: The History Press, 2006.

Hennig, Helen Kohn, *Great South Carolinians of a Later Date*. Chapel Hill: The University of North Carolina Press, 1949.

Journal of the House of Representatives of the General Assembly of the State of South Carolina Being the Regular Session Commencing November 27, 1883, Columbia: Charles A. Calvo, State Printer, 1884

Journal of the House of Representatives of the General Assembly of the State of South Carolina, Columbia: State Printers, 1906.

Lodge, Henry Cabot, *Selections from the Correspondence of Theodore Roosevelt and Henry Cabot Lodge, 1884-1918*, New York: Charles Scribner's Sons, 1925. vol. 1., vol. 2.

McPherson, Edward, LLD, *A Handbook of Politics for 1878 Being a Record of Important Political Action, National and State, from July 15, 1876, to July 1, 1878*, Washington: Solomon & Chapman, 1878.

Moffett, Mary Conner, editor, *Letters of General James Conner*. Columbia, SC: R.L. Bryan Co., 1950.

Morris, Edmund, *The Rise of Theodore Roosevelt*, New York: Coward, McCann & Geoghegan, Inc, 1979.

National Cyclopaedia of American Biography, New York: James T. White & Company, vol. XII, 1904. Contains factual errors re HST including firing at *Star of the West* and Ft. Sumter.

National Cyclopaedia of American Biography, New York: James T. White & Company, vol. XXIV, 1935. Contains factual errors including firing at *Star of the West*.

Sobel, Robert and John Raimo, eds., *Biographical Directory of the Governors of the United States 1789-1978*, vol. 4, Westport, CT: Meckler Books, 1978.

Snowden, Yates, editor, *The History of South Carolina*, vol. V, Chicago: Lewis Publishing Company, 1920.

Thomas, John Peyre, *The History of the South Carolina Military Academy*. Charleston: Walker, Evans & Cogswell Co., 1893

Thompson, Thomas Clarkson, *The Narratives of Thomas Clarkson Thompson, 1860-1938*, edited and annotated by Hugh Thompson Harrington. Gainesville, GA: privately printed, 2019. A copy is in the collection of the South Carolina Historical Society, the Charleston County Library, Charleston, SC, and free download at archive.org., for sale at Amazon.

Thompson, Henry Tazewell (1859-1932), a son of Hugh S. Thompson, *Henry Timrod, Laureate of the Confederacy*. Columbia: The State Company, 1928.

Thompson, Henry Tazewell (1859-1932), a son of Hugh S. Thompson, *Ousting the Carpetbagger from South Carolina*. Columbia: The R.L. Bryan Company, 1927. This book tells the story of this period, from an educated Southerner's point of view. Large parts of the book make for uncomfortable reading to the modern eye. However, read with the understanding that the culture was very different in the second half of the 19th century than it is in the first half of the 21st century, the book conveys a great deal of history and explanation of the viewpoint of the white southerner of the period. Henry T. Thompson dedicated his book to "The Red Shirts of 1876, in every walk of life, to whose unceasing vigilance, tireless energy and exalted patriotism, was due the overthrow of Republican misrule and the Ousting of the Carpetbagger from South Carolina."

Thompson, Henry Tazewell, *The Establishment of the Public School System of South Carolina*. Columbia: The R.L. Bryan Company, 1927. Available online at archive.org and Hathitrust.org.

Wallace, David Duncan, *South Carolina, A Short History 1520-1948*, Columbia: University of South Carolina Press, 1951.

Wells, H.G., *The Outline of History*, London: Cassell and Company, 1920, reprinted November 1934.

Wickersham, James Pyle, *Methods of Instruction*, Philadelphia: J.B. Lippincott & Co., 1865.

Williams, Alfred B., *Hampton and His Red Shirts, South Carolina's Deliverance in 1876*. Charleston: Walker, Evans & Cogswell Company, 1935. This book tells the story of this period, from an educated Southerner's point of view. Large parts of the book make for uncomfortable reading to the modern eye. However, read with the understanding that the culture was very different in the second half of the 19th century than it is in the first half of the 21st century, the book conveys a great deal of history and explanation of the viewpoint of the white southerner of the period.

<u>Newspapers</u>

Charleston Courier (Charleston, SC), February 22, 1856.

Charleston Mercury (Charleston, SC), November 22, 1856, p. 1.

The *Charleston Daily Courier* (Charleston, SC), January 11, 1861.

The Charleston Daily Courier (Charleston, SC), January 16, 1861.

Yorkville Enquirer (York, SC), January 17, 1861.

The Charleston Mercury (Charleston, SC), December 9 and 16, 1864.

Sheriff's Sale, *The Daily Phoenix* (Columbia, SC), November 18, 1869.

Washington and Lee University, *The Daily Phoenix* (Columbia, SC), May 18, 1873.

Richland Rifle Club, *The Daily Phoenix* (Columbia, SC), October 22, 1874.

The Ball, *The Daily Phoenix* (Columbia, SC), February 2, 1875.

Pic-Nic of the Rifle Club, *The Daily Phoenix* (Columbia, SC), May 6, 1875.

The Proclamation, *The Pickens Sentinel* (Pickens, SC) October 12, 1876.

Governor Chamberlain has Issued the following proclamation, *The Tribune* (Beaufort, SC), October 11, 1876.

Latest Wave of the Bloody Shirt, *Yorkville Enquirer* (York, SC), October 12, 1876.

Ballots and Bullets, Thirty-two Companies of Troops in South Carolina, Governor Chamberlain's Letter to the Richland Rifle Club, *New York Daily Herald* (New York), October 24, 1876.

Address to the People of South Carolina, *The Newberry Weekly Herald* (Newberry, SC), October 25, 1876.

Proclamation of the President, *The Intelligencer* (Anderson, SC), October 26, 1876.

The Heel of the Dying Tyrant, *The Weekly Union* (Union, SC), March 2, 1877.

Latest by Telegraph, Grand Ovation to Gov. Hampton! Columbia's Tribute to Carolina's Chief Magistrate! Magnificent Reception Tomorrow, *The Intelligencer* (Anderson, SC), April 5, 1877.

Troops Ordered to be Withdrawn, *The Intelligencer* (Anderson, SC), April 5, 1877.

Gov. Hampton's Return! His Reception at Columbia! His Patriotic Speech!, The *Weekly Union Times* (Union, SC), April 13, 1877.

The News and Herald (Winnsboro, SC), October 26, 1880.

The News and Herald (Winnsboro, SC), October 28, 1880.

The Norfolk Landmark (Norfolk, VA), April 26, 1881.

Yorkville Enquirer (York, SC), May 19, 1881.

Richmond Dispatch (Richmond, VA), June 30, 1881.

Address to Colored Teachers, *The Greenville News* (Greenville, SC), August 21, 1881.

The Intelligencer (Anderson, SC), February 16, 1882.

Department of Superintendence, *The Critic and Record* (Washington, DC), March 22, 1882.

Adger College, Address of Hugh S. Thompson, *Keowee Courier* (Pickens, SC), June 29, 1882.

South Carolina Bourbons, *The New York Times* (New York), August 11, 1882.

Education in South Carolina, *The New York Times* (New York), September 10, 1882.

Governor's Day, *The Watchman and Southron* (Sumter, SC), September 26, 1882.

McLane at Winnsboro, *The Watchman and Southron* (Sumter, SC), October 3, 1882.

The Intelligencer (Anderson, SC), October 5, 1882, p. 2.

South Carolina. A Cool Recital of the Present State of Things. *Chicago Tribune* (Chicago), October 7, 1882, p. 2.

The South Carolina Bourbons, How the Independent Candidate for Governor was Prevented from Speaking at Winnsborough, *The New York Times* (New York), October 7, 1882, p. 5.

The Governor's Message, *Yorkville Enquirer* (Yorkville, SC), December 6, 1883.

Died of Her Injuries, *Evening Observer* (Dunkirk, NY), March 19, 1884.

Keeping Faith With the People, *The Watchman and Southron* (Sumter, SC) [reprint from *News and Courier*], June 1, 1886.

The Abbeville Press and Banner, (Abbeville, SC), [reprint from the *Anderson Journal*], June 2, 1886.

An Appointment Tendered to Governor Thompson, *The Intelligencer* (Anderson, SC), [reprint from the *Columbia Register*], June 3, 1886.

Assistant Secretary Smith Resigns – Governor Thompson to Succeed Him, *Alexandria Gazette* (Alexandria, VA), June 29, 1886.

A Change in the Treasury Department, *The Brooklyn Daily Eagle* (Brooklyn, NY), July 1, 1886.

South Carolina Honored in Hugh S. Thompson, *The Weekly News and Courier* (Charleston, SC), July 7, 1886.

Men of the Hour, The New Federal Appointment, Hugh S. Thompson, Ex-Governor of South Carolina, Made Assistant Secretary of the Treasury, *Lynchburg Daily News* (Lynchburg, VA), July 3, 1886.

Governor Thompson to be the Assistant Secretary of the Treasury, *Newberry Herald and News* (Newberry, SC), July 7, 1886.

Daily News (Frederick, MD), July 27, 1886.

Tents for Charleston, *Courier-Post* (Camden, NJ), September 8, 1886.

The Intelligencer (Anderson, SC), May 12, 1887.

National Republican (Washington, DC), May 25, 1887, p. 3.

San Francisco Chronicle (San Francisco, CA) May 29, 1887, p. 16.

Boston Post (Boston, MA), May 30, 1887, p. 5.

A Revelation to Him, *Detroit Free Press* (Detroit, MI), August 3, 1887, p. 8.

The Life Saving-Service, *The New York Times* (New York), August 23, 1887.

Washington Sentinel (Washington, DC), September 3, 1887, p. 2.

St. Louis Globe-Democrat (St. Louis, MO), September 3, 1887, p. 4.

The Boston Globe (Boston, MA), September 19, 1887, p. 7.

Chattanooga Daily Times (Chattanooga, TN), September 22, 1887, p. 1.

The Grand Island Daily Independent (Grand Island, NB), September 22, 1887, p. 1.

Evening Star (Washington, DC), October 4, 1887.

Smooth Worn Silver Coin, *Fort Scott Daily Tribune* (Fort Scott, KS), May 9, 1888, p. 6.

Blaine's Speech, *Helena Semi-Weekly Herald* (Helena, MT), October 18, 1888, p. 3.

Thompson's Surplus, *The Indianapolis Journal* (Indianapolis, IN), October 20, 1888.

Imposing on the Public, *Chicago Tribune* (Chicago, IL), October 24, 1888.

A Good Man's Good Fortune, *The Intelligencer* (Anderson, SC), December 13, 1888.

Blaine Given the Lie, Hugh S. Thompson Shows the Utter Falsity of the Statements of the Plumed Knave Respecting the Treasury, [reprint of *New York Herald*] *The Manning Times* (Manning, SC), November 14, 1888.

Evening Star (Washington, DC), December 29 and 31, 1888.

Mr. Edgerton Removed, Paying a Private Score at the Public Expense, *New York Tribune*, February 10, 1889.

The Washington Critic (Washington, DC), May 8, 1889.

Evening Star (Washington, DC), October 2, 1889.

Evening Star (Washington, DC) November 6, 1889.

The Negro Question, *The New York Times*, January 21, 1890.

Hampton and South Carolina, *The Washington Post* (Washington, DC), November 8, 1890.

To Help Needy Confederates, *The Baltimore Sun* (Baltimore, MD), November 10, 1891.

The Courier-Journal (Louisville, KY), November 11, 1891.

The Washington Post (Washington, DC), November 13, 1891.

The National Tribune (Washington, DC), April 7, 1892.

Mr. Thompson's Resignation, *The New York Times* (New York), April 18, 1892.

The National Tribune (Washington, DC), December 22, 1892.

Atlanta Journal (Atlanta, GA), January 18, 1893.

The Sun (New York), February 26, 1893.

Omaha Daily Bee (Omaha, NE), February 6, 1895.

The Philadelphia Inquirer, (Philadelphia, PA), March 9, 1895.

Edgefield Advertiser (Edgefield, SC), March 13, 1895.

The Montgomery Advertiser (Montgomery, AL), July 28, 1895.

The Burlington Free Press (Burlington, VT), August 21, 1895.

New York Tribune (New York), July 22, 1896.

The Morning Times (Washington, DC), December 4, 1896.

To the Confederate Dead, Veterans of Both Armies United in Dedication of the Monument at Mount Hope Cemetery, *New York Times* (New York), May 23, 1897.

The Confederates Dine, The Eighth Annual Banquet of the New York Veterans' Camp, *The New York Times*, January 23, 1898.

Southern Society Dinner, *The Sun* (New York), February 23, 1898.

In True Southern Style, Loyal Celebration at the Savoy, *New York Tribune* (New York), February 23, 1898.

Medal for Lieutenant Blue, *New York Tribune* (New York), Jan. 14, 1900, p. 17.

Gift to Southern Society, *New York Tribune* (New York), March 2, 1900.

Honor to Mrs. Jefferson Davis, *New York Tribune* (New York), Jan. 19, 1901, p. 6.

A Tribute to Roosevelt, New York Tribune (New York), September 22, 1901.

Honor Mrs. Davis, Miss Mary Custis Lee Guest at Confederate Reunion, *New York Tribune* (New York), Jan. 21, 1902, p. 5.

Wade Hampton's Funeral, Imposing Demonstration Participated in by More than 20,000 Mourners, *The New York Times* (New York), April 14, 1902.

In Memory of the Dead, The Confederate Veteran Camp of New York Holds Services at its Plot in Mount Hope Cemetery, *New York Tribune* (New York), Jun 2, 1902, p. 4.

The Daily Times (Chattanooga, Tennessee), September 9, 1902.

Gov. Hugh S. Thompson Has Passed Away, A Noble and Lovable Gentleman Gone to His Reward, *The State* (Columbia, SC), November 21, 1904.

Ex-Governor Thompson Dead, *New York Tribune* (New York), November 21, 1904.

Many to Honor Gov. Thompson, *The Greenville News* (Greenville, SC), November 23, 1904.

Governor Thompson to be Buried Today, *The State* (Columbia, SC), November 23, 1904.

Mrs. Elizabeth C. Thompson, *New York Daily Tribune* (New York), July 10, 1909.

Mrs. Hugh S. Thompson Dies in New York City, *The State* (Columbia, SC), July 9, 1909.

Mrs. Elizabeth C. Thompson, *The New York Times* (New York, NY), July 10, 1909.
Washington Post, July 12, 1909.
The Columbia Record (Columbia, SC), January 27, 1913.
The State (Columbia, SC)
Times Union (Brooklyn, NY) September 18, 1925.
The Brooklyn Daily Eagle (Brooklyn, NY), September 18, 1925.

Magazines and Journals

Barnes, Brooks Miles, "Southern Independents: South Carolina, 1882," *The South Carolina Historical Magazine*, July 1995, Vol. 96, No. 3, p230-251.
Heriot, Robert, "Fighting in South Carolina." *Confederate Veteran* 30, no. 11, (Nov. 1922).
King, Ronald F., "Counting the Votes: South Carolina's Stolen election of 1876," *Journal of Interdisciplinary History*, vol. 32, No. 2, Autumn 2001, p. 169-191.
Stokes, Karen, "'Contemplating Desolation': the Early Postwar Life of James Conner," *Carologue*, (publication of the SC Historical Society), (Winter 2016).
Thompson, Hugh S., "The Merit System," *The Century Illustrated Monthly Magazine*, vol. 40, issue 6, New Series vol. XVIII, May 1890-Oct. 1890, New York: The Century Company, 1890, p. 954-956.
Necrology: Hugh Smith Thompson, *The South Carolina Historical and Genealogical Magazine*, Jan. 1905, vol. 6, no. 1 (Jan. 1905), p 44-46.

Other

The Citadel, the Military College of South Carolina, "Minutes of the Board of Visitors of The Citadel, 1861," *The Citadel Archives Digital Collections*, accessed May 7, 2022, https://citadeldigitalarchives.omeka.net/items/show/3 76

The Century Association Archives Foundation. Contains Hugh S. Thompson membership sponsored by Theodore Roosevelt. www.centuryarchives.org

Letter: Roosevelt, Theodore to H.S. Thompson, November 4, 1904. Digital Library, Theodore Roosevelt Center at Dickinson State University: www.theodorerooseveltcenter.org

Letter: Roosevelt, Theodore to H.S. Thompson, May 13, 1902. Digital Library, Theodore Roosevelt Center at Dickinson State University. www.theodorerooseveltcenter.org

Greenville Daily Voice, https://dailyvoice.com/new-york/greenburgh/news/confederate-monument-in-greenburgh-symbol-of-reconciliation-feiner-says/720638/ accessed June 21, 2024.

Westchester Magazine, https://westchestermagazine.com/life-style/is-the-mount-hope-obelisk-truly-a-confederate-memorial/ accessed June 21, 2024.

Letter: Roosevelt, Theodore to H.S. Thompson, April 20, 1897, *The Theodore Roosevelt Papers: Series 2: Letterpress Copybooks, -1916;* vol. 1, April 9-July 12. April 9, 1897, 1897. Manuscript/Mixed Material. https://loc.gov/item/ms382990319/. Library of Congress. accessed June 10, 2024

Letter Theodore Roosevelt to Elizabeth Anderson Clarkson Thompson, November 24, 1908. Theodore Roosevelt Papers. Library of Congress Manuscript Division. Theodore Roosevelt Digital Library. Dickinson State University.

South Carolina Department of Education, Hugh S. Thompson Excellent summary. https://ed.sc.gov/newsroom/former-state-superintendents-of-education/hugh-s-thompson/

National Governors Association. Contains factual errors including firing on the *Star of the West.* https://www.nga.org/governor/hugh-smith-thompson/

1860 Census Federal Slave Inhabitants, City of Columbia, Richland County, SC.

A History of the Calhoun Monument at Charleston, SC, 1886. Published by the Ladies Calhoun Monument Association.

Invitation from President and Mrs. Harrison to Hugh Thompson
and the ladies of his family to attend functions on January
14th, and 18th as well as February 11, 1890, at the White
House. Invitation now in the collection of Joan Harrington
Clayton.